WARHOL'S MOTHER'S PANTRY

21st Century Essays
David Lazar and Patrick Madden, Series Editors

Warhol's Mother's Pantry

ART, AMERICA, AND THE MOM IN POP

M. I. Devine

MAD CREEK BOOKS, AN IMPRINT OF
THE OHIO STATE UNIVERSITY PRESS
COLUMBUS

Mad Creek Books, an imprint of The Ohio State University Press.

Library of Congress Cataloging-in-Publication Data
Names: Devine, M. I., 1978–author.
Title: Warhol's mother's pantry : art, America, and the mom in pop / M. I. Devine.
Other titles: 21st century essays.
Description: Columbus : Mad Creek Books, an imprint of The Ohio State University Press, [2020] | Series: 21st century essays | Summary: "Experimental essays inspired by Andy Warhol's mother, Julia. Provides a literary and cultural history of a new pop humanism, blending history, criticism, and reflection on mid-twentieth-century American pop culture with twenty-first-century popular music, film, and literature"—Provided by publisher.
Identifiers: LCCN 2020020185 | ISBN 9780814256060 (paperback) | ISBN 0814256066 (paperback) | ISBN 9780814278499 (ebook) | ISBN 0814278493 (ebook)
Subjects: LCSH: Warhola, Julia, 1891 or 1892–1972. | Warhol, Andy, 1928–1987. | Popular culture—United States. | Pop art—United States. | American essays—21st century.
Classification: LCC AC8.5 .D47 2020 | DDC 306.0973—dc23
LC record available at https://lccn.loc.gov/2020020185

Cover design by Jeff Clark
Text design by Juliet Williams
Type set in Electra

♾ The paper used in this publication meets the minimum requirements of the American National Standard for Information Sciences—Permanence of Paper for Printed Library Materials. ANSI Z39.48-1992.

ru

who?
lo,
i.c.

my soul

& for mom & pop

: mother to son, son to mother.

see across the centuries. she knows who i am;
i know who she is.

—brian g. gilmore

Contents

3 · A Photograph of a Little Room

4 · The Memory of Film

5 · Remnants, Scraps, Waste: Pop's Postscript

Overture

Acountryisclosingitsborder. Acountryisclosingitsborder.

Another is crossing the water.

A mother is crossing the water.

She has no living children

Acountryisclosingitsborder. Acountryisclosingitsborder.

yet.

(This is not today.)

It's 1921.

A mother is crossing the water.

Pandemic. Persecution.

(The country has no conscience.)

Conscience in every can

Our reputation won't let us make ordinary soups.

We could buy or produce every material we use for a good deal less than it now costs us. And in many cases you might not know the difference. But we know. And the result would not be

Campbell's Soups

She finds flowers there.

(She will have children there.)

Finds flowers everywhere.

(This is not today.)

Conscience in every can

Our reputation won't let us make ordinary soups.

We could buy or produce every material we use for a good deal less than it now costs us. And in many cases you might not know the difference. But we know. And the result would not be

Campbell's SOUPS

Conscience in every can

Our reputation won't let us make ordinary soups.

We could buy or produce every material we use for a good deal less than it now costs us. And in many cases you might not know the difference. But we know. And the result would not be

Campbell's SOUPS

Conscience in every can

Our reputation won't let us make ordinary soups.

We could buy or produce every material we use for a good deal less than it now costs us. And in many cases you might not know the difference. But we know. And the result would not be

Campbell's SOUPS

Conscience in every can

Our reputation won't let us make ordinary soups.

We could buy or produce every material we use for a good deal less than it now costs us. And in many cases you might not know the difference. But we know. And the result would not be

Campbell's SOUPS

Conscience in every can

Our reputation won't let us make ordinary soups.

We could buy or produce every material we use for a good deal less than it now costs us. And in many cases you might not know the difference. But we know. And the result would not be

Campbell's SOUPS

Conscience in every can

Our reputation won't let us make ordinary soups.

We could buy or produce every material we use for a good deal less than it now costs us. And in many cases you might not know the difference. But we know. And the result would not be

Campbell's SOUPS

Conscience in every can

Our reputation won't let us make ordinary soups.

We could buy or produce every material we use for a good deal less than it now costs us. And in many cases you might not know the difference. But we know. And the result would not be

Campbell's SOUPS

Conscience in every can

Our reputation won't let us make ordinary soups.

We could buy or produce every material we use for a good deal less than it now costs us. And in many cases you might not know the difference. But we know. And the result would not be

Campbell's SOUPS

Conscience in every can

Our reputation won't let us make ordinary soups.

We could buy or produce every material we use for a good deal less than it now costs us. And in many cases you might not know the difference. But we know. And the result would not be

Campbell's SOUPS

The flowers all say the same thing.

The flowers all say the same thing.

LOOK!

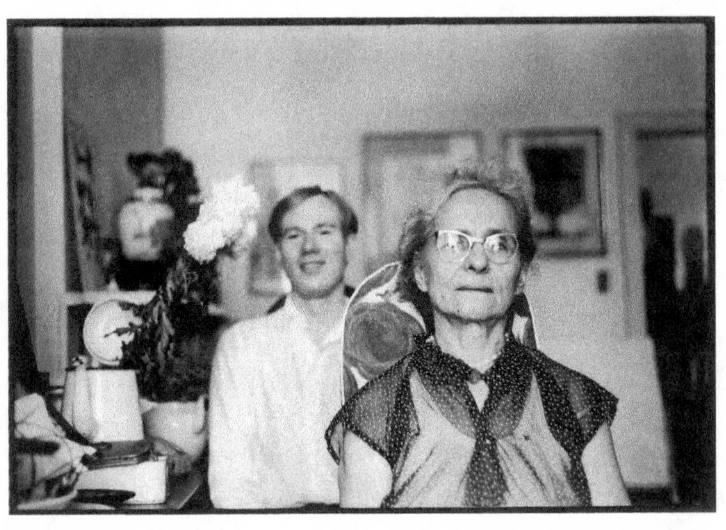

1
The Mom in Pop

Mother Cuts Flowers

On Mom and Pop and Trump Tower

There's a picture of Andy Warhol and his mother that maybe you've seen. He's young, on the cusp of being Andy, famous Andy, but now he's smiling Andy, Andy the unguarded, unshot Andy. His mother, in the foreground, is what gets you: She isn't smiling, but she's not not smiling either. Maybe she looks like she dresses in plastic when it rains, but that's not fair. A straight-back chair with a large flower—a rose?—frames her hair, and it's that flower—the print of a flower—that makes you think about the point and the power of reproduction in her son's work. Origins. The mom in pop, you might say.

A white flower—a real flower—reaches out from the left side of the photograph, and I think of Julia Warhola's first child, an infant girl.

Julia is twenty-one. Her new husband, Andrei, is in America. She's alone in a village in Slovakia and her daughter is dying in her arms. Her first born. Her small hand like a flower, perhaps, reaches up, reaches out.

The bitter fighting that raged in the Carpathians between 1914 and 1916 became as much a war of reprisals on the civilian population as a war between nations. Long-standing, deep hatreds based on emotionally powerful religious and class differences erupted violently and the area was laid waste. Julia's house was burned down and she lost all her possessions. She particularly grieved over the loss of an album containing photographs of her wedding. Andrei's brother George was reported killed by drowning in quicksand as his unit was crossing a river. In a nearby village the fathers of thirty-six families were lined up and shot. As far as Julia was concerned the Russians were as bad as the Germans and the Poles were worse. Her knowledge of the surrounding countryside saved her life.

But many of his supporters found [the death-and-disaster paintings] unacceptable. David Dalton refused a gift of a disaster painting, commenting that he didn't want to have to look at dead people on the living-room wall every day. . . . However, the paintings were soon to make him famous in Europe. . . . "Their subjective quality is neither sadness nor melancholy, nor regret nor even bitterness," the art critic Alain Jouffroy wrote. "The traditional feelings attached to death are banished. In front of these pictures we are cleansed. The paintings become the holy scenes of a godless world."

In 1921 Julia sets out to find Andrei. He's a coal miner. The US will soon shut down immigration from Eastern Europe, and the money Julia borrows from a priest barely funds the journey from the village of Mikova to Pittsburgh. Many have flown before her, escaping war, the European flu: that thought sustains her.

Julia Zavacky comes down to us today as an eccentric accomplice to an eccentric artist well supplied with accomplices—a factory of them, in fact. Famously, she lives in the basement of her son's brownstone during his fame, babushka Madeline, in a way, to the white-wigged Roderick.

But what if, instead, Julia, you signify—your journey, endurance, sacrifice—a human depth upon the surfaces of things, even the surfaces of a son who announces, like Wilde, he has nothing to declare: "If you want to know all about Andy Warhol, just look at the surface of my paintings and films and me, and there I am. There's nothing behind it."

Putting the mom back in pop means finding new depths in Andy's surfaces, perhaps, new takes on his folk forms, his street-level modernism, his ties to an urban culture quickly, quickly going beneath the waves.

Means remembering that Andy was human, and that even Andy way back when thought Donald Trump was kind of a dick.

Disaster: Or, Trump Tower and American Art

The legendary Bonwit Teller Department Store, where Andy made his name designing window displays through the 1950s—along with the likes of Salvador Dalí—was torn down to make room for Trump Tower. A New York fixture, the limestone building featured an entrance likened in the *Times* to a "spilled casket of gems: platinum, bronze, hammered aluminum, orange and yellow faience, and tinted glass backlighted at night."

"A sparkling jewel," according to *American Architect* magazine in 1929.

"Without artistic merit," according to the Trump Organization: The verdict on the building's two-ton Beaux Arts panels helped foreclose landmark consideration and delays in its demolition.

Commissioned by Trump to create a work based on the blueprint of the Tower, Andy writes in his diary:

> *The Trumps came down. . . . I showed them the paintings of the Trump Tower that I'd done. I don't know why I did so many, I did eight. In black and grey and silver which I thought would be so chic for the lobby. But it was a mistake to do so many, I think it confused them. Mr. Trump was very upset that it wasn't color-coordinated. . . . I think Trump's sort of cheap, though, I get that feeling.*

She's a curious muse, I admit—artist, lens for seeing her son (and us) anew. In Pittsburgh, fit with a colostomy bag, she wears her insides on her outsides, scissoring flowers out of empty tin cans of soup and peaches to make a few extra dollars.

> *You take a tin can, the bigger the tin can the better, like the family size ones that peach halves come in, and I think you cut them with scissors. It's very easy and you just make flowers out of them. My mother always had lots of cans around, including the soup cans. She was a wonderful woman and a real good and correct artist, like the primitives.*

A sustainable artist whose spirit teaches us a thing or two about what art contains, how it sustains us, nourishes us; reusable muse, reminder of the virtues of the family size in the age of the individual when everything became something bigger than family size and, at once, much smaller.

Julia, I see you cutting flowers.

Is there a word for something at once big and small in the age of late capitalism?

"Huge"—*yuge*—comes to mind.

Like Trump Tower.

Julia the immigrant, Julia the outsider, Julia the grieving mother, Julia who stocked her pantry full of soup after pandemic and persecution.

Andy, of course, her inflexible, touchy, particular youngest, will be Andy the A-lister, Andy who drops the A, Andy who turns 17 the day the first A-bomb drops, Andygram before Instagram, Andy and the Factory, Andy the Art Marketeer, Andy the Assassinated (almost, day before Bobby Kennedy).

But there's something about that flower—both flowers—in that photograph, and Andy's sly smile.

The smile of the living son who's in on the joke with his mom: He senses something about the wonderful surface of things reproduced—the reproduction of the flower (the son is a reproduction, too, naturally)—and how they point us to the real, the origin. It's art's trick to allow the real to continue, to flower, to endure precisely because the real is always and already so frail, an infinitely suffering thing (by the looks of that flower, stuck in a teapot): a wedding album in a scorched home, death, disaster.

Her son who can't quite say why he does eight pictures of Trump Tower will give himself over to reproductions, copies that function at once as new life and elegy—homages, really—a soup can, a portrait of Marilyn—to redress the slings and arrows, death's blows. Death blows, but pop never quite admits, never quite knows.

⁂

Thinking of flowers—the real and the reproduced—I think of William Carlos Williams, which isn't odd, I think. Reproductions—an obstetrician, babies were his business—fill his poems. Babies, too: "a curiosity— / surrounded by fresh flowers" is how "The Dead Baby" ends, but also how the child begins again, reborn through art, with flowers. New.

Williams has a thing for flowers. In "The Nightingales" he's looking down at a carpet untying his shoes (can a carpet untie your shoes?), and there they are again, "flat worsted flowers / under my feet." It's a quick jot, just a doodle of a poem, a nothing, a note, a poet untying his shoes looking at the flowers beneath him, a carpet, a living room, looking at his fingers, looking at the shadows of his fingers. But why be deep at times like this? Surfaces are enough (if you know how to look). Watch: "Nimbly the shadows / of my fingers play."

Look.

This is not deep. The baby is dead. The movie projector is broken. You're untying your shoes. There is no plot. Things fall apart. This is not deep. But perhaps it's enough. You look at the carpet, like Dr. Williams. You look at the movie screen, like Virginia Woolf. On the screen is a blot, a shadow, a mistake. The projector is broken. See Virginia Woolf believing in the cinema for the first time: "A shadow shaped like a tadpole suddenly appeared at one corner of the screen." She is entranced: Yes, Virginia, this is pop. Beneath you, above you. All around you. The surfaces of things. There are new depths. See the poet's fingers untying, nimbly, untying, now flying, shadows

unlacing
over shoes and flowers.

His body doubles, becomes a shadow, a reproduction, the shadows no more unreal than the flat worsted flowers on a carpet or on a kitchen chair or words on a page for that matter—they are the nightingales. We are the nightingales. The body lives on in that space, redeemed, or at least no worse for wear. Better—maybe even better.

It's there in that space of eternal forms, of nimble movements, where no young daughters die in your arms: there, where we are connected—tied—to each other, to all things. Williams, Warhol, Woolf. Remind me of the surface that has nothing behind it; that has everything; where distinctions are confounded, found meaningless. Help me, Julia, discover new depths.

No wonder Andy is smiling. Perhaps there is something he knows. Perhaps there's something we've missed all along.

And what did Julia Warhola think when she looked into her pantry? Did she remember the daughter she lost in Mikova?

Were the cans lined on her shelves totems of an abundance—32 varieties of soup, Trump Tower—that never quite satisfies, that is "sort of cheap," as her son would say of the rich man who never paid him for his work?

Or did she and Andy find in the reproduced—in the flowers in their lives, the food on their shelves—a dream of sustenance, continuity, possibility?

"Maybe he would get a little baby. I mean a little Andy," Julia would say later in life. Dreaming of her son, the mom in pop sees shadows, nightingales, sons. "All these little Andys, you know, Andys Andys Andys Andys Andys . . . wouldn't that be beautiful?"

She selects a can. She makes soup for her son.

He is happy.

Her husband has died. Fatherless Andy. Andy at thirteen.

She cleans out the can.

Tomorrow it will turn into a flower.

Even Though Leonard Cohen Is Dead

Winter in Montreal and Leonard Cohen tribute concerts have been going since the fall. Each show covers an album. *Songs from a Room* is nice, with old heads and kids with the Ruth Bader specs. Kids with fixed-gear bikes. *Fail better.* Samuel Beckett tattoos. A spoken word concert recording addresses the room:

Let us teach sex in the home
to parents,
let us threaten to join the U.S.A.
and pull out at the last moment

Cohen speaks to his audience and they laugh back then and we laugh right along now with their recorded laughter. The light comes down and we wait for songs that tell us we're not all that free. But it's OK. *The frontiers are my prison. I must do what I've been told.* We'll be one day the audience that's the audience that's not here and that's OK. There's a measure to things and that's the thing we like about songs.

We remember how to sing by singing along.
Whitman wanted great audiences.

Like a worm on a hook
Like a knight from some old-fashioned book

We take our chances.

How Refrains Work

Or, Repeat After Me

Part 1. We Used to Wait

I'm a songwriter, which means I write refrains. Here's one:

A kid just googled
Is God really dead?

Actually, that's only half of it. If you want the rest, you'll have to wait for it.

We used to wait for it. A refrain, a chorus, salvation. That's according to Arcade Fire of yesteryear. "We Used to Wait," one of the more moving meditations on pop form from their sprawling, Grammy-winning *The Suburbs* (2010), seems now the voice of one crying in the wilderness:

We used to wait for it
We used to wait for it
Now we're screaming
Sing the chorus again

Choruses do lots of things. This one condemns and condones. So does Kanye West's "Power": "The chorus is simultaneously boastful, condemning, and anxious." And "How does it feel?" Christopher Ricks on Bob Dylan's "Like a Rolling Stone": "You immediately grant mixed feelings as to how it feels. . . . Terrible, terrifying . . . terrific." In other words, we're disavowed and embraced, punished and pardoned, alone together: this is one function of pop's most powerful form, the ritual refrain.

Hymnals, everyone. Join in singing "Carry On Wayward Son." We thumb our neon bibles. We don't stop believing.

At least that's how poet and critic Michael Robbins makes me see it. His poetry debut, *Alien vs. Predator* (2012), made him synonymous with pop. The poems attempted pop's "formal mimesis," which seemed easy enough to write off as fanboyish, a parodic homage of sorts. But one of the real pleasures in his collection of essays, *Equipment for Living: On Poetry and Pop Music* (2017), is how Robbins tunes us into form as if for the first time. Nas is still there, but so is Dom Gregory Dix going all pre-Nicene in *The Shape of the Liturgy*. Cheech, Chong, Walter Ong. What are these fragments he's Jersey Shored against our ruin?

Or, to echo another Tom (Waits): *What's Robbins building in there?*

Robbins wants a poem to be a pop song. *Can a poem be a pop song?* The question ends a book that upends the usual order of things. Stop asking if a pop song can be poetic, the question that filled your newsfeed when Dylan won the Nobel: "Sometimes his lyrics do rise to the level of poetry" was, for me, the consensus of friends who normally don't attribute to poetry the qualities of gaseous elements. What if that gets it backward? What if, in aspiring to pop, poetry found a new way to talk about its social function, even recovering along the way the pleasures of old-fashioned—no, better—old-school form? Referring to A. E. Stallings and Robbins, Michael Lista has argued that "some of the freshest poetry today is employing some of the stalest techniques." In the face of what he calls pop's "familiar extravagances"—not just Journey wristbands and Yeezus himself, but Axl Rose's codas and more—Robbins makes you wonder: Why refrain? What's stopping us?

For Robbins, "form grounds us in a community, however attenuated or virtual." Those final four words show Robbins—a master of the Twitter short-short form—to be particularly useful for poets today, who, taking the measure of their art and audience, may very well find the "gyre wide af."

That's Robbins's pinned post-election tweet: the core of Yeats's "The Second Coming" ("Turning and turning in the widening gyre / The falcon cannot hear the falconer") in twelve characters you can imagine as easily on a piece of papyrus as on a smartphone. That's consoling. If things do fall apart, the poetic may just survive it all. Call it a Yeatsian repost, a political riposte, or simply good poetic modeling about how form can always be, like everything else these days, hacked: stripped down, streamlined. Hack your life. Hack your phone. Hack a poem, said Pound to Whitman, "now is a time for carving."

Why bother? Because even though "we act like nobody dies," a Thao & The Get Down Stay Down refrain, everyone does. We're alone, and to turn away from form is a turn away from a public tool—equipment—"that symbolically enrolls us with allies who will share the burdens with us," as Kenneth Burke puts it, a thinker useful to Robbins. No surprise, then, that Robbins likes to give props (to Stallings, among others), shout-outs, and even share text messages from friends, but also has anecdotes like this one, from his (sadly) uncollected essay on postmodern poetics, "Ripostes": "I once tried to explain my admiration for Paul Muldoon to a young poet I know, a graduate of the Iowa Writers' Workshop. I opened a book to Muldoon's poem 'Yarrow'; she immediately balked: 'I don't like poems that look like that.' She meant poems written in regular stanzas."

Stanzas carry burdens. One for Robbins is newsflash worthy: "This just in: Everyone you love will be extinguished, and so will you." But the burden is lighter when we can sing along, when we know the song by heart, when somewhere a stranger is singing, too, and we "are linked to him, however briefly, through the public matter of form: an occasion for artifactual embrace." Lighter? "But as I listen to 'Don't Stop Believin'' today, once again, in the arena of my soul, how high that highest Bic lights the dark," writes Robbins (hacking Wallace Stevens).

Robbins doesn't, but I'll quote from *The Princeton Encyclopedia of Poetry and Poetics* on "burden": "c) the leading sentiment or matter of a song or poem d) the refrain or chorus of a song." Burdens are shareable. They are the what and how we share. Reminded of music—of what music does and how it works—I'm again reminded by Robbins of how poems work, of what they do when they really work on me.

Things That Curve and Things You Carry

To discuss form in light of poetry's function seems at this late date to be putting the missile back in the silo. Let's: Robbins makes you want to dream, to remember. "Every song you loved when you were young turns into 'Tintern Abbey.'" What about first poems? I think of the first one that moved me. I read it in a newspaper. It told me what poems do. No, it let me dream about function by telling me about forms, how a poem rings out.

A poem should curve
Like the bell of a tulip
Or a pistol grip
—DJ Renegade

I did what any teenager would do: I immediately tracked down Joel Dias-Porter at a reading—he'd been a DJ, he was a national Slam champ—and asked him to teach me to write. He invited me to a group that called itself the Woodshed. There I worked with brian g. gilmore, Yona Harvey, Ta-Nehisi Coates. I thought these were some of the greatest writers I would ever meet. I was young. Turns out, I was right.

I think of DJ Renegade's haiku when I read, say, about Hart Crane's *The Bridge* and its "inviolate curve," that Aeolian harp, shining like a national guitar. No surprise: It's on that same bridge where Robbins ends his first collection, another poet-DJ remixing the final words of James Joyce's *Ulysses.* Molly Bloom's "Yes" rings out, becomes Robbins's "yes yes y'all."

Is it the rhyme, the alchemy of form (tulips, two lips) that enthralled me? Or the way DJ Renegade says a poem, like something you carry, like something you use, must bend, must curve, if it's ever to work at all? The hook brings you back after all; after all these years it brings me back. Songs bend, curve, hook, return for you in the end. We wait for it. Pray for it. The songs we sing will save our lives, we sing. *Last night*, we sing, *a DJ saved my life.*

Or is it that DJ Renegade's poem states, plainly, that *this* is a handle to grip the world? Equipment. Isn't all of this—poetry's form, function, the way it equips us—central to its political relevance? The poem lives in me. Then and now: Refrains, connects, bridges. Call it the poetic tense, poetic tension, across the decades, across the centuries.

I think of the title of gilmore's brilliant 1992 debut: *Elvis Presley Is Alive and Well and Living in Harlem.* Over twenty-five years later, the dead are still not dead but alive as long as there's a song to sing, a poem to pray. gilmore's newest title pleads in 2019: *come see about me, marvin.* In it he dedicates a haiku to DJ Renegade, whose poem I read in a newspaper so long ago.

Snow is general all over Michigan. Stillness. A setting for haikus. Winter in America. Do we have forms that still we can use? Or are we, as Yona Harvey puts it, "hemming the water"? Trying, trying, impossibly trying: "A woman calls across a continent / & no one answers."

Snow is general all over Michigan. Stillness. A setting for haikus. Winter in America. Do we have forms that still we can use?

cold michigan streets

"black lives matter" sign
nearly covered w/ snow.

gilmore prays to Marvin Gaye. The snow falls faintly on living and dead. Refrains return like a distant lover. We call it equipment because it is.

We call it equipment because of all of this.

But I was a kid. I was a kid. What did I know? What did I know of art's austere and lonely offices?

Part 2. Two Men Meet at the Met

"Wishing Well," a poem off Gregory Pardlo's 2015 Pulitzer Prize–winning *Digest,* floored me when I first heard Pardlo read it. I revisit it and wonder why. The poem tells of a chance encounter between a poet and another man "Outside the Met": nothing special, a meeting, at the Met, with a question—harmless, loaded—about a fountain, about social, communal forms, whether they still exist. What do poems talk about when they talk about forms?

> *and he says pardon me* Old School *he*
> *says you know is this a wishing well?*
> *Yeah* Son *I say sideways over my shrug*
> . . . .
> *Throw your bread on the water.*

The proverb casually tossed. It's the burden of the poem. "Invent a story for some proverb. Which?" thinks Joyce's Leopold Bloom sitting on a toilet, dreaming of authoring a story—a life—with his estranged wife, Molly. "By Mr. and Mrs. L. M. Bloom." For Bloom, texts are useful in all sorts of ways: he wipes himself with the one he's reading. How else? They bind us together. Might literary texts function as "proverbs writ large"? That's Burke in "Literature as Equipment for Living." What's it mean to think about literature in terms of what Robbins calls "shareability"? In terms of application? Burdens?

Perhaps Pardlo's poem moves me, in part, because it stages a refusal to share. His "I eye" isn't exactly an "aye" for solidarity:

> *Because he appears not to have changed*
> *them in days I eye the heel-chewed hems*
> *of his pants and think probably he will*
> *ask me for fifty cents any minute now wait*
> *for it.*

Wait for it. Don't: Because there's no great revelation coming. The world's been cavity-searched, so lose your illusion. Comforting or isolating? "Dom Gregory Dix, in his classic *The Shape of the Liturgy*," writes Robbins, "lamented the decline of the corporate worship of the Eucharist 'into a mere focus for the subjective devotion of each separate worshipper in the isolation of his own mind.'" Well, one can wish otherwise, and "Wishing Well" wants to. Pardlo gets what Robbins calls pop's "artifactual," physical embrace. The rest of the poem is risky, maybe humiliating, cheesy as a refrain you sing along to, a proverb you live by.

It starts with a sign of peace and ends with a refrain: "Hey man I'm going / to make a wish for you too," says our well-wisher, now carrying a coin and a condition. All you have to do is

hold my hand.   *And close your eyes.*

Borderline corny, borderline intriguing. The men embrace ("his rough hand / in mine inflates like a blood pressure cuff") and a burden gets shared: "See now," says the stranger (quoting Mark 8, John 9), "you'll never walk alone" (quoting Rodgers and Hammerstein and everyone else whose heart has touched and been touched by that refrain, from Nina Simone to Gerry and the Pacemakers).

"We have to make ourselves vulnerable to one another," says Pardlo in an interview. "'Wishing Well' moves one to tears," says the interviewer. I guess I'm not alone.

Part 3. What Eve Said

Pop is not enough. Pop is too much. It can be downright embarrassing. Robbins wants a poetry that can rival "its out-scale desire, its extravagant want, its implausible or impossible will." It's the want at the very heart of creation. As my friend Keith Zarriello of The Shivers puts it in a song that reminds you what songs sometimes so effortlessly do, "And then God made Adam Eve / And then Eve said I want more." That's all we want from our equipment, from our poems, from this life. More. Wait for it.

A kid just googled
Is God really dead?
O Siri, can you tell me?
Is it all in my head?

Wear Your Insides on Your Outsides

Part 1. Dylan Wins the Nobel

Poetry can, in a certain light, read like it's pretty much defined against the act of opening one's mouth in public. Since that's what one does when one sings, poetry can, in a certain light, read like it's pretty much defined against the art of songwriting.

In equating poetry with personal freedom, John Stuart Mill hated on ballads. The philosopher of liberty defined poetry as "overheard" (not "heard"), "feeling confessing itself to itself in moments of solitude." Poetry, in other words, if it's anything for Mill, is inward. Which means it's free: free from measures, free from others—audience, listeners.

The Village Voice on how "Bob Dylan Won the Nobel Pretending to Be a Poet": "Dylan began writing more inward-looking songs."

In lots of ways this is wrong.

Also, when poets write outwardly, what are they pretending to be?

Part 2. On Pop, Hip-Hop, and the Norton Anthology, Vol. 1 & 2

We are back in Montreal to see Rostam Batmanglij, the pop architect of Vampire Weekend. Snow piles outside the club. Let's go, my wife says, and here we are.

He sings from *Half-Light* (2017), an album of aubades, let's call it. Predawn songs for parting lovers. "I felt the morning coming through," Rostam whispers on the title track, knowing full well he's not all that free. Not free to stay. Morning's here. One of us must go. Light gets in. "I know, and I knew it / But can't see it, I refuse." Every aubade is written in handcuffs, or might as well be.

We listen to Rostam sing "Sumer." It riffs on the Cuckoo Song, that piece from the start of your old Norton Anthology of Poetry. One of the first English lyrics.

About "Sumer" he says:

> *This song is built over a sample of a choir singing the round 'Sumer Is Icumen In' from 13th-century England. Somewhere in the back of my mind I knew I wanted to make an album that interacted with the history of music. I was thinking about how we measure parts of our lives—in relationships, seasons, sound.*

I was thinking that, too. All winter.

Not the expression of personality, but the escape from it—that's T. S. Eliot on poetry, but I prefer Noname's version, the Chicago hip-hop artist. I find it more democratic. Art as the work of actual human beings. Voices.

He Do the Police in Different Voices. That's what Eliot first called *The Waste Land.* A riff on *Our Mutual Friend* by Charles Dickens, his character Sloppy, all mouth, no head: "You mightn't think it, but Sloppy is a beautiful reader of a newspaper. He do the Police in different voices," says Mrs. Betty Higden, who runs a minding-school, and doesn't mind the boy at all.

Her best boy. Our Beastie Boy. Ad-Rock:

Now when I wrote graffiti my name was Slop
If my rap's soup, my beats is stock

From "Intergalactic": as in dialogic, like an orphan reading a newspaper aloud to other orphans, like a Krylon scrawl on a wall. Ill(iterate) communication? Hardly. Every iteration about our ills; the police; those in power; those who suffer. Our mutual friends: each other. That's what poems remind us we have. Burdens to share. Sloppy, soupy, even, but tough stock. Maybe too much for Eliot, that title; maybe too much. But maybe he should have kept it.

Here's Noname's theory of life, and art, and poetry. Soup to nuts. Like a Whitman's sampler. She's sampling Whitman, the poet who was nurse and printer, typesetter and carpenter.

> *For me, not having a name expands my creativity. I'm able to do anything. Noname could potentially be a nurse, Noname could be a screenwriter. I'm not limited to any one category of art or other existence.*

Her first mixtape was *Telefone.*

Part 3. On Kendrick Lamar

Khalid's "Let's Go" plays as we pour across the border.

Song's consciousness of the other, of tradition—of all listeners, across all time—is its proper subject.

"Promise that you will sing about me," sings Kendrick Lamar, in what Rachel Kaadzi Ghansah calls one of his "blues elegies." Every song is a request, a question, a plea and complaint against time, the ultimate measure.

Let's go. Will you go?
Lassie, will you go?

"Wild Mountain Thyme" is just one more outtake from the Song of Songs: "Come, my beloved, let us go. . . ."

Let us go then, you and I.
In a way it's how every song begins.

Twentieth-century poetry was mostly a desperate attempt to begin that way, too.

Part 4. Only Connect: In Is Not Free

Like the Wu-Tang Clan on their 2014 album (only one pressing made, locked in Morocco [jeweled box], bought by "Pharma Bro" Martin Shkreli), Eliot tried in his way not to be free.

But escaping atomization only proves it. Where have you gone, J. Alfred? A nation turns its lonely eyes to . . . Oh, there he is, in line for Yayoi Kusama's *Infinity Mirror Rooms.*

Take me to church, Eliot finally said, sampling that Hozier song.

As a child I thought W. B. Yeats's "Innisfree" was the saddest poem in the world, a kind of failed transcendence.

I will arise and go now, and go said Lazarus to no one, ever.

You could read the whole thing painted on the wall as you walked into the Irish bar in my old neighborhood.

*In*isfree, it was spelled—though no one ever saw the mistake, they wouldn't have fixed it even if they could.

All Winter I Watch TV and Feel Safe

Part 1. How Does It Feel?

Marie Kondo, do you really want to know?

What sparks joy? Do you really want to know?

Blindfolds. Prison walls. We're warming up to the art of containment this winter. Containers.

Bird Box. Spend a night in the box. Kondo's on Netflix. Warhol's at the Whitney. Society shuts down, but we keep things tidy.

Soup cans and the art of the pantry. When everything is too much, kiss your ugly sweater and let it go. (This, according to my favorite shows.)

Roma, Cuarón's Cleo. The outside is a puddle you mop from the floor.

Pop forms hold us, protect us, shelter us, connect us more than any wall or web, says my TV. Turn off your socials, says my TV. (More and more I do.)

Bird Box. Cultural pivots offer curious allegories, and ours are offering plenty. Straight-to-your-living-room blockbuster releases like *Bird Box* afford, most obviously, the pleasure of listening to mom. Call her Cinemama. Stop talking to strangers. Stop being social. It is a film, in Jaron Lanier's sense (he's pro subscriber-models like Netflix), committed to a kind of cultural deprogramming, curiously attached to the closed door, to riding the streaming service (the river) to an ultimate sanctuary: a school for the blind, a giant bird box, a shared domestic space where eighty million people watch the same thing.

If those who stream together dream together, we're dreaming about our infrastructure in an age of pandemic and plague: that which fails us, that which saves.

But here's the (allegorical) thing. Before the air in the tunnel kills us (socials), the canary sings (pop). It's what the semioticians might call a curious index. It's not a weathervane, not a footprint, but a fragile, dying index nonetheless: its song a song of how there is no air, and that's all that's true, that's all that's real. And the canary sings what pop always sings.

How does it feel?
How does it feel?

Part 2. Infinite Jest (More or Less): Pop Humanism

Strangely, I think of David Foster Wallace. (Wait. Not so strangely; I see in my recommended titles *The End of the Tour.*) He used to call me the idiot box, says my TV. They all did.

True story: After a Kondo binge, I tidy my books. I turn first to a used copy of Wallace's *Girl with Curious Hair,* and read this inscription:

Happy Graduation, Chad
June 9, 2006
Take a class with this guy!
I love you!
♥*Mom*♥

By '08, of course, Wallace is gone. According to my unscientific sense of the "10-Year Photo Challenge" across the socials, that's about the time everyone starts using Facebook. Isn't that what the challenge marked at the end of 2018? A kind of reunion where everyone improbably looked better?

According to Kate O'Neill, author of *Tech Humanist,* the photo challenge (to post a selfie from now and then) helped to train facial recognition algorithms on age progression. Lanier makes similar points in his series of books that lead—to paraphrase T. S. Eliot—from an overwhelming question—*Who Owns the Future?* (2012)—to an obvious conclusion—*Ten Arguments for Deleting Your Social Media Accounts Right Now* (2018). Lanier thinks, when it comes to this kind of media, we do not ask what is it—but we should. "Behavior Modification Empires." That's his name for the socials, their contribution to a feeling that things are always and only darkening. If you want things darker, there is always James Bridle's *New Dark Age: Technology and the End of the Future* (2018).

Anyway, I didn't get far cleaning.

I think of Chad and his mother, and open Wallace's collection to its first, expressionless page: a child and his mother in a movie theater. 1970.

"The child's eyes enter the cartoon. Behind the woman is darkness." Out of the darkness a man "leans forward. . . . He plays with the woman's hair, in the darkness."

Whose hand reaches, I wonder, for the cinemother?

I think of Wallace, his ten-year challenge, Mary Karr and #metoo.

Did we ever really believe in the death of the author?

I make room on my shelf for Hanif Abdurraqib's latest work in pop criticism (and love), *Go Ahead in the Rain: Notes to A Tribe Called Quest* (2019). It's a book for our moment, in part a series of letters dedicated to making visible the pop infrastructure by which we (once?) oriented our lives. He writes here to the late rapper Phife Dawg's mother, the poet Cheryl Boyce-Taylor: "I know what it is be a son and long for a living mother."

Ours is a moment for pop elegies, which, actually, is a sign of vitality. A shuttered nation, everything viral: Bob Dylan releases his elegy for Kennedy in March 2020.

Dead Kennedys. Late rappers. Living mothers. The elegy is the barest and best expression of a pop humanism: an act of address—an homage, a soup can, a portrait of Marilyn, a letter to Phife's mother—to redress the slings and arrows, death's blows. Death blows, but pop never quite admits, never quite knows. Call it childish. Call it garish. Call it faith. As Franz Wright once wrote, "In my opinion you aren't dead. / (I know dead people, and you are not dead.)"

Writing to the rapper's living mother, Abdurraqib lets me recover hip-hop and him—Phife, my boyhood hero—in a new way. I think of my old *Low End Theory* tape, machines with buttons that said "play."

I think of Julia Warhola's pantry.

Some byzantine Byzantine icons, perhaps, her son's soup cans: his mother an immigrant whose first child—an infant girl—died in her arms in a village in Slovakia.

We're putting the mom back in pop.

Part 3. Watching a Prison Break TV Show, I Think of Warhol

Pop won't fail us, perhaps we believe, if we make it visible, appreciate it for the fragile, dying, human thing it is—a sign and measure of our search for sustenance. Why not call this Pop Humanism?

Our new Warhol. He draws by hand.

He's like the prisoners in Ben Stiller's *Escape at Dannemora*, yet another allegory about infrastructure and clear vision in the age of streaming. To see clearly behind prison walls—the escapees practice a crude hand-drawn pop art—is a means of discovering a new route (a heating pipe) to freedom. Warhol, too, provides a map of the infrastructure by which we truly come to know each other.

Of course, retrospectives tell us more about now than then. Warhol's drawings, says Philip Kennicott, "advance the project of humanizing" the artist who said, "I want to be a machine." The Whitney calls this the "Warhol before Warhol," but let's call him Warhola, the immigrant's son, his drawings—our pop culture—an index of our exile, what sustains us, where we call home.

His mother's pantry, her insides on her outsides; the messy fact of interior matters, that interiors matter: pop traces our fragile social bonds, and we're valuing that now, perhaps more than ever.

Part 4. Door in the Floor: Pop's Infrastructure

Infrastructure, obviously, is boring. If it weren't it would get in the way. I think of this as I stream Alfonso Cuarón's *Roma,* its slow panning shots, its undramatic domestic interiors through which (mostly) women come and go.

Pop is reclaiming its space in our lives, in our homes, and that's a good thing. *Roma* marks this, commemorates where we stream together, where we are connected, and watch, and learn to see, as if for the first time.

"I consciously tried not to pay homage or do anything derivative," says Cuarón, in yet another act of cinematic deprogramming.

Unflinching, we watch her stillborn child and Cleo, like Andy watching a sleeping John Giorno. Warhol's first film: *Sleep*. Five hours long. Like Julia watching her sick child sleep. Like your dead father laid out in your living room. A wake. Awake, unflinching, we watch Cleo and her stillborn child. Like Julia watching her sick child.

The stillborn child we watch, and watching we become patient as a machine and as silent, learning from the cine-mother the calculus of homage and elegy.

What are these rooms where we stream? Where we discover, like prisoners, a source of warmth, a heating pipe, a lost infrastructure that may very well connect us and save us?

Aren't we merely watching atomized and alone, welcoming a new dark age each in our cell, as Terrance Hayes puts it in his "American sonnet," "part prison, / Part panic closet, a little room in a house set aflame"?

Maybe. Maybe not. I sort through books. On TV there's crying. I can't bear to look. Does this spark joy? Kondo asks a couple in a condo. Does this spark joy? I'm trying to ask the same. Imagine a different life. Imagine a spark. Imagine the flames.

Dead Poets

Part 1. For Lycidas Is Dead, Dead

For Sam (you are not dead): my friend

I had a friend. He died in _____.

I had a friend. He died in _____.

❧

O, Caroline Levine, tell me what this can possibly mean.

> *If we were interested in containers and enclosures, then why not analyze prison cells? All of these were designed arrangements—deliberately crafted to impose order—just like art objects.*

❧

I had a friend. He died in _____.

Caroline Levine, is this what you mean?

> *One of the places where humans have some agency is in the orders that we ourselves impose: our spatial and temporal arrangements—our* forms.

I had a friend.

I can't begin.

Part 2. Had Ye Been There

Thanksgiving I hear.
Dylan is on and I am in the kitchen. I remember a song. It is asking a question.
"Who Killed Davey Moore?"

We hadn't spoken for a year or more.
Everybody's talking how badly they were shocked. I can't find _____. The dead are an echo in your mind.

All winter long I write a song. Not this, not this (but I might be wrong). ~~*You cross things out.*~~ You start again. It's a nice thought: to start again. Winter. Wasteland. Remember how much we read back then? We met in grad school way back when. Old school. Reading Hart Crane. Summer never surprised us. (This was LA.) T. S. Eliot. Remember how he began? *He Do the Police in Different Voices.* Wasteland. Wasteland. It's a nice thought: to start again. But I don't know how. And it's not true.

I hide in stalls. I dream of rooms. Empty grows every bed. I dream of saying just one word—that that is all that must be said.

I dream I'm in a Sister's cell: a nun's I used to visit. Religious. Religious. I'd make my visit. A child. Her room. Her room. (Old candy in a cookie tin.) My father's father's sister's sister. Don't be scared: go & kiss her. In her habit at her funeral. Don't be scared: go & kiss her. (My grandfather's sister was a Sister.)

Why do I dream of her?

All winter I watch TV and read and dream. Dream of her room, the forms she chose. The shape she poured her life into. I feel boxed in. All winter. I think of you.

Let us go and make _____. I can't. If I had a hundred years and more and weeping, sleepless, in all that time I could not make good. Said Berryman. Or Milton. Who could?

I hide in stalls. I read the walls. *I was here.* ~~*So was Red.*~~
(A writer wrote. A writer crossed it out in red.)

Everywhere elegies: I read them all. Refusals. *I was here.* I read them all. *Fail better.* Samuel Beckett tattoos. Refuse death. Refuse failure. Kids with Samuel Beckett tattoos. *Ever tried. Ever failed. No matter.* Fixed-gear bikes and fixed-gear bike tattoos. And *Fail better.* A Samuel Beckett tattoo. I read them all. I think of you.

No one tattoos

> *Know better now. Unknow better now. Know only no out of. No knowing how know only no out of.*

Kids with Samuel Beckett tattoos.
I want to unknow better now.
Show me how.

⁂

It is impossible to say just what I mean, thought Jesus, as he tried to explain.

> *Lazarus, our friend, has fallen asleep. But I am going there to wake him up.*

"Lord," said his disciples (they were new to his parables), "if he sleeps, he will get better!" (It is impossible to say just what I mean, thought Jesus, as he tried to explain.)

Perhaps God so loves the world He gave his only son. Perhaps. But perhaps we'd be better off if the signs said

John 11:14

("He told them plainly, 'Lazarus is dead.'")

⁂

No.
To speak is to dream is to unknow better now. You have fallen asleep, my friend. Like John Giorno, who died yesterday, October 12, 2019. The beautiful boy sleeping in Andy's first film, *Sleep*. Five hours of John asleep. John was a poet and now he's asleep.

Then he returned to his disciples and found them sleeping. "Couldn't you men keep watch with me for one hour?"

I can. Like Andy. Like Andy. Like Andy's mother watching her sick boy sleep. I am not Jesus. I can't speak plainly. I've wept and fasted. Write and wait. Give you what I cross out. These mistakes. This way of unknowing better. I write for you to wake. I wait for it. It's how I keep watch. It's how I wait.

Rhyme recovers the body, I've read. Returns what once you thought had fled. Though different. Hopkins, the Jesuit poet: Rhyme is "the proportion of disagreement joined with agreement." Limits: It makes me feel those. *Jesus, don't cry.* Radio consoles. Radio consoles. I turn the station. I've locked myself inside: these lines. How I mourn, still mourn. I repeat to choose to feel how it feels to lose.

That final arrangement. That rough design. That last little room. My friend did not choose. This end. My friend.

I watch and wait.

Let us begin.

Part 3. Who Would Not Sing?

The thing that you see that you did not see when you were young in "Persimmons" by Li-Young Lee is not just violence—"In sixth grade Mrs. Walker / slapped the back of my head"—or that there's defiance; it's how repetition refuses, refuses silence (even after she slaps your head)

> *for not knowing the difference*
> *between* persimmon *and* precision.
> *How to choose*
>
> *persimmons. This is precision.*

Imperfect, the slapped boy who cannot pronounce. But he refuses silence. Keeps saying the word. (He's a poet.) And the refusal is the poem, and it's imperfect, the poem, like the boy, and it's perfect, scattered, like this, like memory.

You taught me that poem. We practiced teaching like children playing at teaching playing. Playing professor. (If we were lucky, lecturer.) *Mon semblable. Mon frère.* Was modernism even modern or just police and despair? Hard to tell. We read Baudelaire.

The poem's about plosives, you said. Pressure builds. *Feel it in your mouth.* The shape, heft of words. (Heft: voiceless glottal fricative.)

Hold the word inside your mouth, you said. *Practice. Precise. Persimmon.* Mouth is a little room. Open the door. Pa. Pa.

> *My mother said every persimmon has a sun*
> *inside*

Mother repeats, too. I see that now. Teaches her son, bears him, carries him. Like Julia, like Andy. Mother repeats, too.

We read Hart Crane together. Do you remember? What does time slay after all? Not the boy I see in Li-Young Lee repeating, refusing, choosing. Not you, not you, who taught me that poem.

So many mysterious poems: I search them all. They tell me, I guess, that you're not there. But you are.

Have you practis'd so long to learn to read?

We did, didn't we?

Have you felt so proud to get at the meaning of poems?

We did, didn't we?

Tell me, Walt Whitman, where are we going? I've practis'd so long. What if a poem, this equipment for living, a word, is all I have? To bring a brother back.

You shall not look through my eyes either.

Then whose, Walt?

Whose?

So many mysterious poems: I search them all. They tell me, I guess, that you're not there. But you are.

I listen to the radio and think of Hart Crane, again: *The phonographs of Hades in the brain.* I understand. I finally understand. Poor Crane. Poor Hart. Beneath the sea his body went. "O, hypermnesic unleashing!" Derrida? Joyce? Crane? It's hard to remember: *the hook brings you back,* I think is all it ever meant. An old refrain. It all brings you back, my friend. Every song. Poem. Refrain.

~

John Milton. He wrote to recover his friend, Edward King, his Lycidas, dead at twenty-five. Poet and scholar. You were thirty-four. Dead, dead. *His gory visage down the stream was sent.* It's hard to remember: *the hook brings you back,* I think is all that Milton ever meant.

~

I have a prayer to pray, says every blues traveler, a sing to shay, says Berryman. Unburied, Milton wrote to recover his friend, unburied, alive as long as there's a poem to pray.

how old am i? today, i'm today.

Danez Smith: another poet's prayer, so many to share. If you were here. Milton wrote to recover his friend: *His gory visage down the stream was sent.* And Hart Crane, he was dreaming of Lycidas, he was dreaming of Poe, Poe at his end, how poets end, over and over with pop on his phonograph, or maybe Ravel's *Bolero,* Hart writes of how poets end, of Poe at his end, and you know the rest, you know the end, of how it all ends:

I often meet your visage there
They dragged your retching flesh
Your trembling hands that night

~

Lead me Underground, my friend, my Lycidas, my heart, my Crane. The subway section of *The Bridge*. Remember, together, we read that part?

> *Or can't you quite make up your mind to ride?*
> *The subway yawns the quickest promise home.*

⁂

Shall I go? Let us go. (How could I know we'd all meet there?)

> *Fight was what I did when I was frightened,*
> *Fright was what I felt when I was fighting.*

The boy in that poem understands. This confusion. This violence. This love.

O, life.

How could I know we'd all meet there?

Mon semblable. Mon frère.

Part 4. At the Door

I read a review of Anne Carson and it makes me think of you. *Nox,* her book about her dead brother. *Nox,* her book about Catullus and his dead brother. *Nox,* her book about translating the Latin poet's poem for his dead brother to elegize her dead brother. Catullus is a dead poet and his poem for his dead brother is now simply called "Catullus 101." Like an intro. Like a primer. Like a class you take you don't want to take. Like an intro to brothers in boxes. "Soaked with tears of a brother / and into forever." Books are boxes, too. Carson's is. The classicist: her book packaged in a box like a school kid's old-school Latin primer, like exercises in translating, in remembering. "It contains bits of uncollected memories and discarded dissolutions. It even has some lines of poems." Old school.

> Nox, *which means night in Latin, is a box.* Nox *is a box with two dead brothers and a book inside.* Nox *is a box with two dead brothers. Anne Carson stores life into a knowable poetic space, one of the definitions of lyric poetry. And then she protects that space in a box. As if night itself could be kept in a box.*

I read a review of Anne Carson and it makes me think of you, which means it makes me think of me.

I want to tell you about something that happened before. When I looked into a box that kept night inside. I never told you this. And this is the only way that I can begin. Listen.

I was, I'm told, a beautiful boy.

They took my picture. Said be still. Be the Little Drummer Boy.

And that was hard. You tried. You cried.

(But everyone agreed: it was the best Christmas card.)

—

I modeled for drawing. Near the museum. Carried an arrow and bow. I never told you this. About the city. When I was older: skateboard kids in Love Park. Kids like kids in *Kids,* that movie by Larry Clark. They were so easy. So cool. So free. (Knocked me down. Scared me.) Reading Latin on the subway, scholarship to the Jesuit school. Fourteen. Dead poets and me. Virgil, Catullus. Always had a thing. Read my brother's college books. Whitman, a bridge you take to Camden? My brother's notes: "*stock still*" underlined, careful annotation. "*This is alliteration!*" Always had a thing. Under Philly. On the subway. Tell us, Catullus: What was it all for? Did you have a brother you could not save? What would you tell him? *Cui dono lepidum novum libellum?*

—

I never told you about the boxes. How as a child, they could not keep me from them.

Mother, sister, inside the museum. Lose me in a Warhol kind of wing. Bright. So new. Wondered if they were empty. Brillo: red, white, and blue. You'd look at all the sides to see. Cubes.

Cubism, honey. Cubism, see?

—

But here's a secret I never told: They were only how I knew that I was close to what I'd really come to see.

> *It occupies a closed-off room in a dead-end area at the back of the main Duchamp gallery. The room can't be entered. The entrance is blocked by a pair of locked antique wooden doors, solid except for two tiny side-by-side peepholes in their center.*
>
> —"Landscape of Eros, Through the Peephole," *New York Times* (2009)

According to Louise Glück, "At the end of my suffering / there was a door." I'm not so sure. But at the end of the Duchamp gallery there was a door. I remember that. A dead end. A room you can't go in. (In my mind I still come to see.)

Later, older, I'd read and reread the parts from which Marcel Duchamp built it, the cell called *Étant donnés: 1° la chute d'eau / 2° le gaz d'éclairage . . . (Given: 1. The Waterfall, 2. The Illuminating Gas . . .).*

They found it constructed inside his studio. He was gone. About suffering, the old master took so long, from the Second World War on, to understand its human position. To build a box. A body holding a lantern. A room. As if night could be kept inside a mere cell.

A body (dead?) inside that room? Why? What was it all for? Two peepholes: I put my eyes against the door. In my mind I put my eyes against the door.

Open one and close the other. Open one and close the other.

See if what I see repeats. It doesn't.

You do it again.

Left [then] right

I investigate my incompleteness. Is art just seeing? Feeling being. Is that the thing? Seeing our seeing: thinking, thinking how do we account for what we know we are missing? Teaching us how to unknow better now? Is that the thing?

Later, older, I'd read and reread the parts from which he built it—like a home turned inside out, its insides on its outsides; the piano in the living room ripped apart; tool box emptied; pantry, too.

wooden door
iron nails
velvet
hair
brass piano hinge

and, listed near the end, a

cookie tin

In my mind I stand outside that cell again, my Lycidas, my friend. Sometimes it is Duchamp's and I am inside a museum; sometimes a prison cell, a prison cell. But most often, I am in a convent.

My father's father's sister's sister. Sister. A nun. (Old candy in a cookie tin.)

I am seven. Ten?

This is her room. This was her room. Now she is gone. Stand at the door where she locked her life in.

Don't be scared.

Look in.

Part 5. Look Homeward, Angel

Given:

1. Dead Nun's Room
2. My Two Eyes Looking

The nun's room was like a ransacked chapel,
clean and bare. It felt as if no one was living
there. There was no evidence of choice or taste,
no private mess to spill on things nearby. It's not
strange, they slept, the dispossessed, like _____
(I'd try the windows, try)
(painted shut, nearly died)
(bedpost, a scapular): there's so much more
I can't quite bring to mind. So much less is
known than unknown. Those we leave behind . . .
From their perspective, of course, they leave us.
But we move on, the distance distorting
the dead

beyond recognition. How quaint it all can seem:
(how useless). Piano in a living room, alone
since no one sat down to play. Tradition:
never having to miss the past. Is it
always only now? When did she choose
no longer to decide to choose? How? Was she
burdened by choices she would lose? A life pent
in . . . pews and classroom aisles? No,
each day—a thing well-made. Strong shape, more
to pour a life into . . . What? Is this choosing?
Mother will be laid to rest. Brother will, too.
Me. Me and you.
The dead. They are an echo
we turn into.

Part 6. Still Morn

None of this is true. But maybe it is.

In 2003 two boys meet in LA. That is me. And that is you.

Forty years before, October 1963, an old man—the old master, Marcel Duchamp, pop's pop, pop's pop-pop—has a secret. He's standing in a hall. He's being fêted! He has a secret. Party for him, pop's old master! His first retrospective! Someone ask him his secret! (He's building a room, a box, inside his studio. No one knows. It's his secret.)

(I am not there, of course, but maybe I am. My friend, my Lycidas, you understand: I was not there. But maybe I am.)

And there's Warhol, see him? Andy's first trip to the coast: LA. Sat in the back; let others drive; looked at the signs.

See them there: They meet. They talk. Warhol, Duchamp. October 1963. They are still alive. We are still alive. They talk. In the rooms the artists come and go, talk of, what? Brillo, Brillo.

No. No.

I think of you and dream they speak of being slow.

Marcel is building a box to keep death inside.

And Andy is making a film, his first. He will call it *Sleep*. They speak of being slow, of visions and revisions, of bodies, and of elegies. Let us listen in.

None of this is true. (But maybe it is.)

Duchamp:

> *I think there is a great deal to the idea of not doing a thing, but that when you do a thing, you don't do it in five minutes or in five hours, but in five years.*

Andy:

O.
—*I think there's an element in the slowness of the execution that adds to the possibility of producing something that will be durable in its expression.*
—O.
—(whisper) *I'm building a room. With a body inside. You look in. A leg. An arm. Perhaps she holds a mirror. You look at you.*
—O. I am, too.
—*I want to do what film used to.*
—O. I'm making a film. It's about a sleeping man. It's as long as the night. Things that don't move help the audience get more acquainted with themselves.
—*She holds a mirror, perhaps. But I'm not sure. A lantern?*
—The sleeping body helps the audience get more acquainted with themselves.
—*She holds a mirror, perhaps. But I'm not sure. A lantern?*
—The sleeping body helps the audience get more acquainted with themselves. You could do more things watching my movies than with other kinds of movies; you could eat and drink and smoke and cough and look away and then look back and they'd still be there.
—*You're right. She won't hold a mirror. She will hold a lantern. The audience must get acquainted with themselves. With incompleteness.*
—My mother used to sit by my bed and watch me sleep. I was sick as a kid. She was patient as a machine. When you're watching you become patient. Leave a little light on. She would leave a little light on.
—*I will call it*
—*Sleep.*

Part 7. Genius of the Shore

Farewell, John Giorno! Stock still and now asleep. You died in October, yesterday, in fact, and a leaf turned red, in fact! Leaf! Don't be neurotic! (Who was that? O'Hara? Farewell, Frank O'Hara!)

Giorno! Farewell! Koestenbaum says you let Andy perform "his filial wake" in *Sleep*. His first film! Poor Andy, scared of his father's dead body: Andy, thirteen and hiding, hiding upstairs. A three day wake! A five hour film! Farewell, Andrei Warhola! Giorno, take your waking slow!

Farewell, Duchamp! You spent your life building your Black Maria, that early cinema studio. We see death in the peepholes! Life! Black Maria! Edison's first movie studio named after the paddywagons! Police! To think! Police and despair! What can we never arrest? Time! No! Did you build it for me? (Hair and velvet and a piano's insides. A cookie tin? A cookie tin! You raided the pantry! You raided the pantry!) You dropped the mirror, Duchamp! Teach us how to look at things! Did you let Andy show you how?

Farewell, conversations that happened, that might have happened, that never happened! Dead poets! Farewell, Lycidas! I see you now! On the shore! I see you all! I had not thought, death. No. So many more! Still they come in droves! My friend, my friend!

Twenty-eight young men bathe by the shore! Whitman! Eakins! Philly! No, more. More! Forty-two! More! Like in that painting by Bellows. See them dive from docks into a green century! And what should I tell them? The flock! They dream of jackknives, nosedives, cannonballs! Our bodies are bellows, made for clocks; prayers are rocks tied to balloons. But here, now, see something unlocked: like Muybridge's horse, something you follow like a dream of whole motion! I am here. I am at the door! I am at the shore! See you, Lycidas, see you splash in the water! Not drowning. Waving! "Stock still" as Whitman's twenty-ninth bather, as Bellows's forty-third! I see that you are all but one, all but one Word. I am still, stock still. O, watch out for the rocks! I am still, stock still: on this frame's dark edge, this page, this broken dock!

Farewell, Hart Crane! May no one ever paraphrase you! You were right after all! Though it all can often seem illegible—the Word made flesh, the Word made digital—there are moments when the surface of things becomes permeable, and the poem, which proves nothing, proves there is nothing unimaginable! Untranslatable! Indivisible! We are but one. One Word.

I feel I am with you. I am with you in prison. Inside the museum. Inside the convent. I feel I am with you. I am a child. I am at the peephole. I am at the door. I feel I am with you. I am in LA. It is 1963. It is today. I feel I am with you. It is 2003. And I am right now. How old am I today? Today I am today. I feel I am with you. I am complete. I am never complete. My friend, my friend! I am complete. I am never complete. I am never complete. I am never complete.

Am I?

2
Repetition and Redemption

Self-Contained

On Gisèle Freund

You've probably seen her pictures but never her. Here, Gisèle Freund captures herself, she who was never captured, escaping wars, escaping Europe, that which sought to contain her self. She's self-contained, of course, hand before her heart, hand on a trigger. She's in Mexico City. 1950s. But she's thinking, I think, of the 1930s. From Frankfurt where she studied with Adorno, Benjamin, she developed a name, an eye, a talent for reproducing a world, a Europe that is going away, going away.

I think of Virginia Woolf at the movies: "The Cinema," her essay about film's power to preserve, to contain. The past. People forget because it's easy to forget. In 1926 "The Cinema" shows up in a New York City arts journal first. The Cloisters just opened. Medievalists brought churches back to the States and called them art, museums. The past, and so what?, is something you make.

What does it hold on to, that which we reproduce, that which we save? What did Andy's soup cans remember? His mother?

Virginia Woolf is at the movies. Bored but then she's not. She likes mistakes, shadows on the surface of the screen, a speck in the shape of a tadpole, the shape of "fear itself," she calls it. Watching old movies in 1926. Movies from before the War. People laugh at the past. The audience laughs at the past that they turn into.

But Woolf does not laugh. She writes:

> *We behold them as they are when we are not there. We see life as it is when we have no part in it. As we gaze we seem to be removed from the pettiness of actual existence. The horse will not knock us down. The King will not grasp our hands. The wave will not wet our feet. . . . Further, all this happened ten years ago, we are told. We are beholding a world which has gone beneath the waves.*

Beneath the waves: Freund stood on the coast, too, sensed the sea change, the end of something. In the face of this she sought to capture, to reproduce, to save what she could.

She's known for capturing Woolf herself, who even "agreed to change her clothes to see which best suited the color harmony." You've probably seen them: pictures of waxen Woolf against a blue couch, Woolf with flowers and fabrics, Woolf's hands arranged like something from Klimt, like so many modernist hands (Georgia O'Keeffe's, say). This, and then, in a year, the London Blitz: "Basement all rubble. Only relics an old basket chair." Exposed, transformed, redeemed, perhaps. How does one talk about the reproduction of the self, about what Freund was saving as she captured, shot, contained these artists?

Freund specialized in a special kind of repetition, a Joycean kind, and of course she captured him who hated to be captured for the mass media market: *Time*, in 1939, world at the end of something, maybe at the end of time.

Joyce, like John Donne's God, would rather not submit, would rather not be contained, but he did (he was injured during the first photo shoot; Freund's camera broke; Joyce swore in front of her, felt guilty, invited her back, finished the shoot).

Contained, reproduced, repeated. Susan Sontag's "inventory of mortality"? Not here. No limits. "The inexhaustible panorama of the human face," Freund called it. #nofilter. Her own portrait oddly bisected. A mistake? No matter. This is an actual human being, we feel. Reproduced. Freund knew that something was gained and not lost through the image, the repetition, just as Joyce's simple words repeat and in repeating open up new vistas.

What do we gain and what do we lose when we surrender to the limits of language, its repetitions?

Why do we prize originality when all we want in the end is to endure?

I think of Andy who let his mother sign his checks, sign his paintings. I think of Andy surrendering. Unoriginal Andy. Andy and Julia.

The Doodler Abides

On James Joyce (feat. Eimear McBride, Jean-Michel Basquiat, and Andy Warhol)

Part 1. A Reader's Guide to *Ulysses*

If you've never read *Ulysses*, here is one thing you really need to know:

1. "All" appears often—very, very, very often—in "Penelope," the book's final chapter about Leopold Bloom's wife. People think it's important that "yes" ends the book, and yes, it is, but it's not all that matters. "All" does. The affirmation of everything. That anything can be contained. That art can hold everything. Hold us. That words can, too. Can, do.
2. OK. Two things. You might also want to know that haters hated on this used-up all-containing allness of its reproduced, repeated language.

D. H. Lawrence: "My God, what a clumsy *olla putrida* James Joyce is! Nothing but . . . cabbage stumps of quotations . . . what old and hard-worked staleness, masquerading as the all-new!" Geeking out, we might counter Lawrence by checking out Stephen Dedalus's first composition in *Ulysses*, evidence that all writing—consciously, unconsciously—roots through the cabbage stumps in the garbage. The young poet, believing himself original, actually repeats Paul de Kock (nice name, that; real pop writer, Bloom's taste) and even Percy Bysshe Shelley. The word "pale" in Stephen's poem is proof. Garbage pails, thought Lawrence; garbage pales in comparison—to what? Originality? The all-new?

Remember, art critics, the antique land of the 1980s. See Rosalind Krauss run circles—grids, really—around the myth of originality. "'Originality' is a working assumption that itself emerges from a ground of repetition and recurrence." Boxed in, artists desire to be original, and so they paint . . . grids.

"Highly inflexible," Krauss notes, though "a prison in which the caged artist feels at liberty." Original? All-new? Same old? Is there not another way? What does Joyce have to say?

Read Joyce and see how things get used, repeated, consumed. When you conclude, you might conclude, at the end, he tries, in his way, to not be free, but you're off the grid. Way off. (You're home.) True (who knows?): Freedom is a masquerade, mummery. A memory. But the things we use in the pantry are the things that endure. That's why they're there. That's what we use them for.

3. Here's the third thing to know, maybe the most important: Molly ("Penelope") is where we must journey as readers, writers, artists, don't-stop-believin' believers. Like Warhol's mother, she's an artist. Let her bestow upon you inheritance. Lay down your weary tune. Shake off the sense that you are an individual, original. Understand your connection—to, well, all.

(*Ulysses* is about the journey to that understanding. To understanding repetition. To understand: Play. Doodle. Dawdle. Take time. Delay. Like Molly, Julia, Penelope.)

Part 2. In Bloom

Leopold Bloom makes an observation that is so straightforward it almost escapes notice. "Beauty of music," he reflects, "you must hear twice." The goings-on at the Ormond Bar, the memory of things past, the songs, the tears in beers: The comment seems true enough. When the book sings, refrains, Joyce gives counsel. Reader, it's here. Take note. It's here.

Why not listen? Why refrain?

Pop is the language of many, a word that holds, contains, sustains.

No wonder Joyce repudiates the Romantic conceptions of language and authorship held in his earlier work.

Stephen Dedalus, on his way to the MFA, had a great fall. Who pushes him? All. All of us.

All words are used words, Stephen will find; they cart histories like a girl for whom time's gone wrong, leaving Slovakia, house and home; arms spilling over, junk and treasure. Every word, an urge, an urge, a social energy that defies. Possession.

What can we ever possess? What can we call *mine?*

The book is full of echoes and clichés, alive, living, pointing back, forward to some common anonymous fund. See "Lestrygonians," the butcher shop; look at "the suspended carcasses of dead animals" hanging like some Damien Hirst exhibit. Reader, pass by, leave death behind. To "Penelope" move on: the end, where the simplest words repeat, repeat, shape-shift, defy.

Father-mother, says the infant (who has no words), it's impossible to say just what I mean. Then repeat after me, sweet child o' mine. This public resource of language is, no more or less, the inheritance that Odysseus-Bloom bestows on Telemachus-Stephen, the socializing force of father-mother. It militates against the individualist claims of the child.

(Pop is what the parent gives the child, the child a repetition, too.)

Child must come into that inheritance, that identity. Diminished?

No, enlarged.

Part 3. Words Suck

Before "Proteus" the only repeated word is the persistent description of Stephen as "quiet."

From quiet, from silence, Stephen and all of us must travel, like Telemachus, to inheritance.

Stephen is cautioned to surrender: this he cannot do (yet)—but in time he must, to language, pop. Like Seamus Heaney will ("When you have nothing more to say, just drive"), Stephen learns how to on the coast, where he sees in words a silt-like quality—residual, accumulating:

> *Before him the gunwale of a boat, sunk in sand. . . . These heavy sands are language tide and wind have silted here. . . . Hide gold there. Try it.*

Once he could draw forth "a phrase from his treasure." Nothing outside of him. How different things are here. Stephen dreams of pop: prodigal son, his rightful inheritance, pop's treasures (mom's, really).

Portrait of the pop artist according to Warhol: Andy reminds us to merely like, celebrate, use, and reuse the things that we like, the things that serve us.

Try it. You have some.

On the pages of *The Tyro*, T. S. Eliot: "Whatever words a writer employs, he benefits by knowing . . . the *uses to which they have already been applied*. . . . The essential of tradition is in this; in getting as much as possible of the whole weight of the history of the language behind his word." There are limits to words, liminal edges, like the coast you see almost everywhere when you're on an island (say, Ireland). The edges are historical, they are history: the coast a space of contest, colony, crucible. Have you read Heaney? His coast is "water and ground in their extremity." It is history and language, and those things, well, they suck. The sand Stephen walks over is “the suck.” Suck: the first word—sound, action—you make. Infant: without speech. And it’s what troubles young Dedalus when he hears it used as a derogatory term for a classmate in *Portrait*: “Suck was a queer word. . . . The sound was ugly.” Unhinged, almost transformed years later, suck is now the sand, the “silt.”

Silt.

> *These heavy sands are language tide and wind have silted here.*

History. Accumulated but not buried: language. We walk upon its surface.

Does the artist dig, or rather scratch the surface?

Bloom writes a message on the sand, “I AM A . . .” (lover of the surfaces of things). *Amo, amas, amat.* Latin, *love.* Scratching, scratching, doodling, scrawling.

No need to be deep.

Here’s Eimear McBride, our new Joyce, and much more: Behold, a portrait of the artist as a two-year-old. Behold, connoisseur of carpets (worsted flowers), couch legs. The doodler abides, the doodler abides:

> *Flowers on. Leaves for green. The couch leg I drawn red biro in the grain. Digging. Singing long long ago in the woods of Gartnamona I heard a blackbird singing in a blackthorn tree. Oh. That’s come from. Come from where? I can’t remember any before.*

The girl in *A Girl Is a Half-Formed Thing* (2013) is repeating: who? Heaney, sure (“The squat pen rests. / I’ll dig with it”), and yet her (blood) red pen will later return as weapon and hammer for the hands and feet, lance for Christ’s sides. (This is all very un-Heaney; very un-Bono; very #metoo; very un-U2).

At church, later, she colors a hole-y picture, doodling wounds on the sly. The doodler abides, the doodler abides:

> *I thought Christ was his second name. . . . Drawing blood down between his legs.*

Little girl's Jesus period.

Portrait of the Artist as an Irish Girl Hiding in the Pews.

Non serviam. I will not serve. Stephen gets redeemed; even Stephen gets reused.

A new icon, a kind of defacement. Byzantine, camouflaged, like Warhol's late period: *Camouflage Last Supper* (1986). Every repetition, in McBride, an opening of wounds: "I met a man. I met a man. And wash my mouth out with soap." Like Stevie Smith with scissors, the repetition cuts through. One hundred years after Joyce, the Irish writer still cuts through. What? History.

History in *Ulysses.* It can suck you in. In McBride, it sucks, it sucks, it sucks you in.

But it's also a song you remember to sing. You can't remember a time when you didn't sing along, and in the song there's a bird and the bird is singing, too.

Part 4. Breakfast with the Built-In Bounce

A (not very) serious question: Has there ever been a proper history of the doodle? Doodling as a scratching of surfaces, a playing upon, purposeless, playfully repeating.

Well, when it comes to doodling, don't ask what is it. Go and make your visit to the news offices with Bloom, the advertising agent. There the machines "Sllt. Almost human the way it sllt to call attention. Doing its level best to speak." The *silt* again, the symbol of history, language, now the primal suck, public energy, a kind of song, rhythm, if you listen. Pop. Like Lars von Trier's *Dancer in the Dark* (2000). Listen. You're in a factory, but it's almost like *work* wants to rhyme with *Björk.*

"Thump, thump, thump." Listen. Bloom does. In "Aeolus," turned on, like a pop artist, Bloom feels the energy of the newspaper printing machines at the *Evening Telegraph.* Unyielding, machines are writing, and doing something more (and less): "Now if [the foreman] got paralyzed there and no-one knew how to stop them they'd clank on and on the same, print it over and over and up and back. Monkeydoodle the whole thing." A dream of paralysis. Not the worst idea, considering. Considering what? History.

The news office, home to the borrowed phrase and the pat formula, like Bloom's mind, like Joyce's book, goes *sllt,* reminds us of the *silt,* history. Language. *Sllt* contributes to it: the sound of machines repeating, and in repeating becoming almost human. The repeating is a doodling, isn't it? Isn't it? For Joyce, it's a nothing, nonsense: childlike, unadult, inhuman, animal, monkeydoodle. It's art.

Modern art wondered, pop wondered, Rosalind Krauss wondered, Joyce wondered, Warhol wondered: Might we become almost machine? Is that what we do when we doodle? Isn't that what we do?

Doodle. A form of repeating, writing, drawing, mindless (well, less mind, more body). A form of redeeming, maybe? Redeeming what? The body. In Jean-Michel Basquiat's hand, doodling as *defacement*—elegy, homage. *Defacement*: that's the word on his painting, *The Death of Michael Stewart* (1983), though it's defaced, too. He scribbled the whole thing on the wall of Keith Haring's apartment, in memory of Michael Stewart, a graffiti artist killed by police. The word "defacement" itself defaced, the second *e* erased, blotted out, a blot like the body of the Black man in the doodle.

(Haring removed the drywall, put a gold frame around it. Look. Art.)

This is pop, the scratching of surfaces. Surface stuff. Superficial. *Super.* Latin, *above, beyond.*

And(y) Warhol? He remembered Stewart, too. Like Bloom, he simply reprinted the newspaper page reporting on the death, buried somewhere in the potter's field of the *Daily News.*

Artist could have been choked: doc

Further tests on the body of a graffiti artist who lapsed into a coma and died after he was taken to Bellevue Hospital by police show the man's blood flow and breathing were restricted by a force like that of "a choke hold," a physician hired by the victim's family said yesterday.

Tests were performed on the eyes, neck tissue, brain and spinal cord of Michael Stewart, 25, of Brooklyn, who died Sept. 28, two weeks after he was taken to the hospital.

Last week, city Medical Examiner Elliot Gross said preliminary autopsy reports indicated Stewart died of cardiac arrest. Further information would be presented to the Manhattan district attorney's office, Gross said.

Attorneys for the victim have alleged Stewart was beaten by Transit Authority police. Police have denied the allegations, saying Stewart became violent and had to be restrained.

Dr. Robert Wolf, an internist and cardiologist at Mount Sinai Hospital hired by the family to monitor the autopsy and tests, was present Monday at Gross' office, which conducted the additional tests.

Wolf said the tests showed that Stewart had sustained a force like that of "a choke hold." A final report on the autopsy could come in about 10 days, Wolf said. Gross' office had no immediate comment on the latest tests.

Brandt joins nuke protest

Bonn (Combined Dispatches)— Nobel Peace Prize laureate Willy Brandt will join the tens of thousands

25% 25% 30% 25% 30% 30% 25% 25% 25% 30% 25% 25% 25% 30% 25% 25% 25% 25% 25%

25% 30% 33% 25% 25% 25% 25% 25% 25% 25% 25% 25% 25% 50% 50%

"Artist could have been choked: doc," reads the narrow left hand column. The column chokes Stewart, the colon chokes the meaning: Doc? Documentary? Document? Doctor? Undoctored, this document on the doctor is a pop documentary.

The right hand column: a list of percentages, an advertisement to let you know that things—belts, blazers, bras—are—30%, 25%, 50%—off. This is art stripped down. Warhol's gloves are off.

What does one column have to do with the other? Are these sales? Or probabilities?

The likelihood the police choked to death a Black man doodling? Place your bets. Don't hold your breath. Art here is choked, passed out, defaced like Stewart—pop as paralysis, like Bloom's foreman at the machine.

Print it over and over and over and over, those WarholJoyce-Basquiatdreams.

Thump, Thump, Thump goes the night stick, the bass line, the boys in blue, the bottom line, the printing press, the heart attack, the transit cop, the broken neck.

Ж

A Word from Our Sponsors

And just a quick thought about breakfast cereals and injustice.

Do you think the two are unrelated?

Watch this commercial.

[Voice-over]

On the eve of the pop revolution (Andy still Andy the ad-man: 1950s crushes, ambitions, drawing shoes, selling, shelling), Jasper Johns, the artist, is watching TV. It's 1954. He wants to make something special. He will. He wants to make something everyone will see. He will.

Twelve Angry Men is on.

Twelve Angry Men is on TV. Jasper Johns is watching TV.

In a muggy jury room, not many lines to speak, not a saint, Juror 12, an ad-man, speaks up:

> *Mmm? Oh. [He holds up the doodle.] It's one of the products I work on at the ad agency. Rice Pops. "The Breakfast with the Built-in Bounce." I wrote that line.*

Twelve Angry Men is on TV.

See on the screen a doodle of a box of cereal. Juror 12 holds it up. A boy's life is on the line.

I have this habit of doodling. It keeps me thinking clearly.

Not many lines to speak, not a saint, Juror 12, an ad-man, speaks up, thinks clearly: the jurors sit around a conference table, like the one he sits around at work.

He has, he says, "a quick thought."

A quick thought about justice.

Maybe the jurors should all say why they're right and Juror 8 (the one holdout, reason, American principles) is wrong.

He's right. The burden. The burden of proof. He's thinking clearly. This is justice. Doodling. It's just a quick thought.

Not many lines, not a saint, an ad-man, Juror 12, the doodler speaks up, thinks clearly.

Repeats lines from his office; repeats American ad-execs; repeats the darndest things. Repeats. Repeats what ad-execs like to say:

Here's an idea. Let's run it up the flagpole and see if anyone salutes it.

Jasper Johns is watching TV.

Stupid expressions, tired expressions, the darndest things. Repeated lines. Repeated images.

This is pop. Joyce's *silt. Sllt.* Repetition.

It calls attention.

> *Here's an idea. Let's run it up the flagpole and see if anyone salutes it.*

This is pop. Joyce's *silt. Sllt.* Basquiat's defacement of Keith Haring's wall.

It keeps us thinking clearly.

Here's an idea. Let's run it up the flagpole and see if anyone salutes it.

Jasper Johns thinks about the flag. Jasper Johns thinks about the flag.

Jasper Johns thinks about the flag. Jasper Johns thinks about the flag.

It's just a quick thought.

Part 5. Writing on the Toilet

One of my favorite moments in the book: Bloom's aspiration to write a sketch like Mr. Beaufoy, whose story, "Matcham's Masterstroke," Bloom reads and admires before he "wiped himself with it." In "Circe" Beaufoy reappears to accuse Bloom of having "cribbed some of my bestselling copy, really gorgeous stuff, a perfect gem, the love passages in which are beneath suspicion." Beaufoy's slips here ("beneath"!) reveal yet another plagiarist.

But what I most like is this: Bloom's sense of language as a public resource. Bloom-on-the-toilet ponders a possible writing career:

> *Invent a story for some proverb. Which? Time I used to try jotting down on my cuff what she said dressing.*

Jot down. On the cuff. Or off. Just a quick thought. This is pop, the mom in pop. What are proverbs? Language strangely used, worn, passed through, unscathed: Throw your bread on the water. Comes back. Message intact. Despite repetition and through repetition the proverb continues to masquerade as something new. Mummer. From thinking of proverbs to Molly the muse: Bloom's consciousness of literary creativity always, always leads him there, and us to "Penelope." There, repetition of the simplest words; there, the dream of freedom springs from a mind that prizes the social, the used, the consumed.

All. All.

Julia Warhola.

Part 6. Come, Come, Come

See the slaughter of sacred ideas of authorship and origins in "Scylla and Charybdis." Stephen still wants to be the artist-individualist, still needs to challenge the anonymity of authorship, the doodlers, the advertising agents, the machines, us. (He still needs to grow up.)

His task: a lecture on Shakespeare's personal relationship to the creation of *Hamlet.*

But alas.

The myth wobbles, hardly supports itself; the originating father becomes not one but many.

> *When Rutlandbaconsouthhamptonshakespeare or another poet of the same name in the comedy of errors wrote* Hamlet . . .

Owners are multiple; he's growing up; maybe, he gets it. Now the comedy sets in: "They talked seriously of mocker's seriousness." Monkeydoodle begins at home (or at least with the Bard).

More?

"Come" and "Come to me": what is sacred and profane, what is serious, sexual, and silly in the novel. All, more or less. Come, comedy.

"Come": first Bloom's mysterious instruction to Stephen in the dream that he recalls in "Proteus"; Molly next uses it—Bloom overhears her—as a playful instruction to the cat: "Come, come, pussy. Come."

The triangle that each future "come" will conjure: Molly, Stephen, and Bloom caught in an interplay of "comes" sexual, mystical, romantic.

More? More. The "Come to me" of Mary the Blessed Virgin enters Bloom's mind. His meditation coincides with the finale of *Martha*:

> *Bluerobed, white under, come to me. God they believe she is: or goddess. . . . All comely virgins.*

All must come.

Come all ye faithful.

Finally, a climax (of sorts): Bloom's meditation corresponds with the moment he realizes his chance to reclaim paternity:

> —Come . . . !
>
> *It soared, a bird, it held its flight, a swift pure cry, soar silver orb it leaped serene . . . high, of the high vast irradiation everywhere all soaring all around about the all, the endlessnessnessness* . . . .
>
> —To me!

Consumed, reader, you, too, are invoked: you've been singing along after all, audience, artist, what's the difference.

> *Come. Well sung. All clapped. She ought to. Come. To me, to him, to her, you too, me, us.*
>
> —Bravo! Clapclap.

You take a bow.

Part 7. A Little Molly Goes a Long Way

Humans are frail: Molly's sleeping with Blazes Boylan, *totes epic fail* (as kids used to say in 2010).

But Bloom seems to think he shares her with all of humanity, so what's the big deal? (That includes you, reader.)

Or Molly does. In what way is unclear. Is she a figure for language? A resource shared? A sustainable muse, "endless" in service of meaning, whatever that means? Is she a printing press? A monkeydoodler?

It's a dirty process, to be sure. To Lawrence, remember, it's garbage, it pales in comparison: to what?

Is Joyce's epic, to repeat, an epic fail?

No. Stephen finally realizes it: "Sounds are impostures." It is only then when Stephen and Bloom gain successful entrance into the abode of Penelope-Molly, the unmatched hub of play, creativity. Place of Pan. Call it the Pantry. In "Penelope" words sound twice most frequently; the repetition of what is most simple reveals the strange "beauty" even in the mouths of fallen, fallen humanity.

Fallen?

Here's Molly on her doctor:

> *And asking me had I frequent omissions where do those old fellows get all the words they have omissions. . . .*

Which brings us back to "all," Rule #1 for reading Joyce's book. Molly's simple words forge a cosmos of quick thoughts—doodles, really—where nothing is out of bounds. Nothing is omitted. Everything is visible. Out in the open.

Out?

Hear Molly recall her struggle to get a marriage proposal "out of [Bloom]"; Bloom burns "the bottom out of the pan all for his Kidney"; men drink "champagne out of her slipper after the ball was over," and, of course, pull children "out of her."

In and out.

In and out.

In and out.

Urge and urge and urge: to wit (to Whitman), the knit of identity. What art holds, how it holds us, and what it finally reminds us of is this: limits, yes, and the all that is always and already possible.

God in a Can

On John Donne (feat. Kendrick Lamar)

Part 1. Can Words Hold God?

Question: What do words hold? What can they not contain? Can they hold God?

Ask John Donne.

Eternal God—for whom who ever dare
Seek new expressions, do the circle square,
And thrust into straight corners of poor wit
Thee, who art cornerless and infinite—
I would but bless thy Name, not name Thee now

John Donne's rare (noticeable) moment of poetic reticence. To get all 1970s about it, Donne's reluctance to name God brings to mind Jacques Derrida's point about names: "A name is a proper name when it has only one sense. Or rather, it is only in this case that it is properly a name."

I think of Julia Warhola in church. She's praying for her son who's changed his name. He wants to be an A-lister.

You might say it's wise, then, to keep God from entering the fray—language—which always threatens to destabilize one's capacity to establish presence. Why stop there? As safe, say, to keep God away from Warhol's camouflage stage (*Camouflage Last Supper*, 1986, his final days), Eimear McBride's bleeding ballpoint pen. Donne, I think, is aware of this threat. He's what I call a spiritual schizophrenic (he'll be fixed with a few pathologies, we'll see). He who wants to bless but not name Thee.

Tricky.

What does art contain? What can it hold? What should it not hold? Can we can God?

Can we? Can God?

Can God what?

Part 2. Speaking of God

Being God is tricky, right?

It's a difficult piece of diplomacy, somehow "being made present" to humanity in a way that does not compromise the exercise of our will. This is what's been called "presence."

I demonstrate.

Sit in adoration of the Eucharist. I used to do this. Youngest of seven. (Julia. Andy, too, sometimes, did you know?) Is God alone? I wondered. After Mass. Churchgoing. The quick are gone, now the slow. You'd think that absence is one way to know for sure there's nothing going on. You're wrong. It's when I loved the most. The quiet deepened like a coast.

What can we ever possess? Hard to ever say what's *mine.* Am I?

Art helped to establish that presence. Once. Carpentry and cults. Dappled things. Some stained glass window my son can't comprehend. Donne reminds us of many things—of a split, too.

Donne, Catholic born, then Dean of St. Paul's some twenty years after he left the church of his family, has—what do you call it?—Catholic guilt.

Donne's God respects the right his creatures have to resistance. For this reason a unique plane is built by which God achieves presence to dwell closer with the ones he loves. This plane, in Donne's thought, is language.

(Don't tell Derrida.)

ᚷ

Check out Donne's *Essays in Divinity.* The topic "Of the name of God" leads Donne to debate the relative dangers. On the one hand, he concludes, any attempt at naming "signifies as much the essence, as we can express." But things get more interesting in a section titled "Prayer." God, Donne first labels a "power," is realized on more human terms as "an Active guest and domestic" seeking presence in his creatures:

> *For Thou hast said, 'I stand at the door and knock, if any man hear Me, and open the door, I will come in unto him, and sup with him, and he with Me,' and so Thou dwellest in our hearts; And not there only, but even in our mouths; for though Thou beest greater, and more remov'd, yet humbler and more communicable than the Kings of Egypt, or Roman Emperors. . . . Thou hast contracted Thine immensity, and shut Thyself within Syllables, and accepted a Name from us.*

God's great, and how tricky. So is Donne. God seeks to "dwell," but Donne wants—needs—to make the point that this is in our hearts. That's all. But not so fast. Upon further review, the receiver—or maybe God—was out of bounds. God was in your mouth, turns out, all along. (That's not as odd as it sounds.)

Donne can only attest to God's desire through Jesus's words. Knock, knock, says the door. Not heaven's, the heart's. How to answer? Donne stutters: God needs not language (or does he?), but does so in the spirit of humility to reside "even in our mouths." Contained, humbled, imprisoned. Syllables "shut" in the immensity of God as if they are walls. It is this dimension, this verbal containment, this very desire to be in our mouths like food, like sustenance, that haunts Donne's writings.

We can God. (Weekend, God, we do. Sundays. We chew. We chew.) God's in our mouth after all. A weakened God?

Now here I'm spitballing:

Donne, of course, asserts God's freedom—being "humbler and more communicable" than all secular kings. Containment is a free choice, a surrender, love, the kenosis of Christ, the human touch. Nevertheless, it's undertaken due to human bidding.

OK. Donne doesn't explicitly say whether God exists outside of language. Perhaps because Donne so loves the wor(l)d that he just doesn't care. Like Hopkins, he reads in the Book of Creatures the unmistakable authorship of God. But undone, always undone is Donne. He has to complicate things. God is a strange king. And so hard to know.

> *Certainly, every Creature shows God, as a glass, but glimmeringly and transitorily, by the frailty of both the receiver and the beholder.*

☧

Little Eyes: Or, Kendrick Lamar and a Glass That Shows God

Kendrick Lamar is worth citing here, and perhaps Sunday services would be more popular if he were cited there, too. Let's see what he says, quite literally, about how we are seen in this world we're passing through. In his song "i," his lyrical "I" repeats this image of scriptural surveillance, the miraculous mirror that is anything but. On its surface there's a blot. A shadow. A smudge. Or maybe it's worse than that. Much worse. Funhouse mirrors. Mirrors are in police stations, too.

"I know God," the rapper starts off, which is risky business (1 John 2:4), dangerous stuff to assert. You can get killed for that. Crucified. Unless. Unless the world is upside down, like the world is upside down in his video "Alright." (Actually, he is, floating, topsy-turvy, upside down, in the crowd, above the crowd, now he's standing on infrastructure, lamp posts—Is he our infrastructure? Is that what will be alright?—he's a modern Chaplin, maybe, for these modern times, why not?, with the crowd bearing down on us, he's a Christ-figure capable of flight. Or is it fight? You always forget in the heat of the moment.) Reversals, trick mirrors are what Lamar is all about.

A lot gets packed in a little, no doubt. Like maybe he's not an I at all but an *i*, which is maybe a ♥ if you squint at it a bit.

Try.

The single's release put the signs like this on its cover. Is it the Trinity?

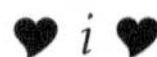

But the hearts in the photo—go look it up—are made by the hands of men. Bloods and Crips. Gang signs. Red and blue. Colors. Like blood. Like what blood looks like on the outside and the inside, when you wear your insides on your outsides.

Hieroglyphs, this world. Hard to get a grip. That's what Donne's saying, I guess, and Lamar, too. Especially when you're not an I at all, but a *me*, an object, like God in a relationship with his creatures, like God who can hardly be seen.

More Lamar:

> *In front of a dirty double-mirror they found me*

This mirror isn't Donne's, of course. It's Paul's (1 Corinthians 13:12), the famous letter writer:

> *For now we see through a mirror, in darkness, but then we shall see face to face.*

And the line goes on, loops us back to the start of "i" after all. This is how Paul's blurred vision ends, in a new kind of self-knowledge. Am I complete? Not yet. But I will be.

> *Now I know in part; but then shall I know even as I also am known.*

"I know God," like Lamar says from the start. And maybe we can, too, if we have a heart. If only we know him—Lamar, the poet, the Word. Can we? Hard to see it happening. The mirror is dirty, double, reversed, policed, reflecting a culture of eye for an eye. No, worse than that, much worse. Fallen, cursed.

But not beyond redemption, according to Lamar, reusing Paul, reusing John. Even the Psalms: "Be still, and know that I am God."

Hard to be still when you're treated like fodder, so you keep moving "at meteor speed," Lamar raps at meteor speed. Of course, all is fodder to hip-hop anyway, according to Ta-Nehisi Coates: it's what makes it "sonic democracy." But maybe it's more. Maybe it's sonic theology.

Give "glory to the feeling of the holy unseen," Lamar finishes, unfinished. Theology of the invisible, of the wholly unseen. What's it all mean?

All is fodder, says Donne, to God the Father. Look around. See your father.

> *Certainly, every Creature shows God, as a glass, but glimmeringly and transitorily, by the frailty of both the receiver and the beholder.*

Lamar says that, too.

But the creatures are blind, poor close readers. Hieroglyphs. A man's hand in the shape of a heart. An *i*. An eye. What's it all mean? Says God, says his creatures:

> *When you lookin' at me, tell me what do you see?*

In the beginning was the Word. And that's when the trouble started.

The world is the world. Poor parchment. Poor parchment. One more reason why Donne's God has to use words, our mouths even, to establish presence. Good luck.

We're only human.

Part 3. Bulimia and Other Forms of Prayer

Here's Stanley Fish: "The object of [Donne's] desire and of his abhorrence . . . words, and more specifically, the power words can exert." Words pop, create energy, but what frightens Donne is just that. It's precisely that: The same capacity to "bring referents into being . . . undermines the claim of [the] producer of signs to be real, to be anything more than an effect of the resources he purports to control." What we talk about when we talk about Donne talking about God, in other words, is language (and vice versa, and vices, and verses).

Donne is the spiritual schizophrenic. In *Sermons,* a common meditation is on God the creator, and particularly the one who creates through language. This God leads to some of Donne's trippiest flights—raps, really—in meteor speed.

Sermon for the day: the incomprehensible disparity between God and his creatures. A cypher on a cipher, call it: about our black thought, our overleaping pride. But can you blame us? Donne's freestyle mesmerizes, multiplies, and bridges the divine.

> *But shall man, between whom and nothing, there went but a word,* Let us make Man, *That Nothing, which is infinitely less than a mathematical point, than an imaginary Atom, shall this man, this yesterday's nothing, this tomorrow's worse than nothing, be capable of that honor, that dishonorable honor, that confounding honor, to be the enemy of God, of God who is not only a multiplied Elephant, millions of Elephants multiplied into one, but a multiplied World, a multiplied All?*

He (Donne) went there, elephants and all. And in going there—reducing humans to nothing; wait, check that, a nothingness that exists on a temporal plane stretching from yesterday into the foreseeable future—the effort is undone. Donne's own admission: God's generating verbal act creates some space "between" nothing and humans. But once Donne testifies to the power of words, you just can't deny it. The creature turns to creator and employs words—no, re-creates, plays, raps, cyphers, doodles, draws cartoons, whatever—to make God an elephant. An elephant!

(Making Jesus—follow me, you who thirst—the Elephant Man.)

But that's the breaks; for God, that's the game. Your love means you're subject to that verbal power by which you stake your claim as creator.

You can almost feel, as the kids say, the burn.

Of course, Donne doesn't want it that way. God, "a multiplied All," is desperate to flee the realm of signifying, but can do so only by means of, well, language. Infinite movement of metaphors in which God can never be located. That's what's in your mouth: a serpent's tongue.

"So Man is an enemy of God."

But not just that.

Another sermon: "God made us with his word, and with our words we make God." Former Catholic—full of guilt—merely wants a sacramental sense.

Don't we all? But to make is to unmake. To chew is to swallow is to spit out. No wonder Fish calls Donne the verbal "bulimic."

PART 4. FLEA

Frank Kermode writes it off as a poem that "enchantingly demonstrates" how "the highest powers of the mind are put to base use." No longer bulimia, just scopophilia. In looking at the Book of Nature, Donne studies the teeny, the tiny, the flea. His sense of all. Awe. His poem "The Flea," naturally, is about the Trinity.

Kwame Dawes tells us that Bob Marley was thinking about the Trinity: "Three Little Birds." Three little words. And Rodin, sculpting his three nymphs dancing, all from one cast? Was he thinking of the Trinity, too?

But the flea is more obviously the Trinity precisely because it is one: a receptacle for the mingled blood of two lovers as well as its own, trinity of Donne's making. It's a model for the wooer wanting to make it with the wooed. Here's the math that adds to three:

Mark but this flea, and mark in this,
How little that which thou deniest me is;
It sucked me first, and now sucks thee,
And in this flea our two bloods mingled be

It's not sound logic, but it sounds like logic. No "sin, nor shame, nor loss of maidenhead." It's nothing. Nothing will happen if you play the game, the wooer promises. But something has happened when God wasn't looking. The "diminution" of God that Donne warns about in "Expostulation XIX" has come to pass. But it's not so bad. It's a way to play, to pass the time. To woo, to wonder. To kill the Trinity by squashing it with your thumbnail.

Easy.

⚜

There's so much drama for Donne the former Catholic. No more sitting in adoration; instead, in our mouths we hold the real, the Word. The power of language that repels and attracts bulimic Donne—the way God the houseguest wants to be ensconced, leaving us at wit's end (ensorcelled, entranced, our mouths an entrance)—is part of the beauty, the insanity, the grandeur of his work. Lamar's, too. We want God. We want more.

And God?

God only wants to be loved. He steps into a word, a container, a cabinet. A pantry, say.

A mouth. A tabernacle. Churchgoers. Going. Gone.

He hopes for the best.

The lights click off and the dark clicks on.

Reading Poems with Scissors

On John Berryman (feat. Tyehimba Jess and Leonard Cohen)

Part 1. Scissors Are Scary

"Cut, cut, cut nice."

That's Julia Warhola, lady of the tin cans cut into flowers. She's remembering her son, remembering how little Andy "cut, cut, cut nice." Boy genius with scissors at seven, lord of the comics, movie mags, boy who rends, removes, excises, exercises control.

✂

You cut to save things, liberate them, heal them, too. They cut your mother: "Cut out Julia's entire bowel system and replaced it with a bag on her stomach." Experimental procedure. First time for everything.

Boy reads with scissors in hand. Mother cuts flowers from cans. You can. Do.

✂

Scissors are scary. Was it Elaine Scarry? A tool makes; a weapon unmakes, she said. Sometimes hard to tell the difference.

✂

Scissors trouble poets. The old master Tennyson "said he knew the quantity of every English vowel except those in the word *scissors*." This, from R. P. Blackmur in one of those canon-making essays—*the* canon-making essay—from 1951: "Lord

Tennyson's Scissors: 1912–1950." Pound, Yeats, Eliot. The New Critic's Holy Trinity, we're told, knew what Tennyson meant (whatever he meant). The masters, old and new, unite meter and rhythm, "see things bound together."

Strange, you'd think scissors would cut. But no. Bloodless, bodiless, no longer a threat to the Lord, these are mid-century modernist, which is to say, magic scissors. Poetry lets us hear, do you hear it?, the "music of Lord Tennyson's scissors." Blackmur says poetry is a game we play with reality. Of course, criticism is, too.

✂

You might as well know this, too. Just about the time of Blackmur's essay, in a boring English office, a woman, not so young, with promise, perhaps, mostly behind her—a startling literary debut, derided, dismissed (flapper lit?)—is personal secretary "to an underemployed son of a publishing magnate." Watch her. She picks up Lord Tennyson's scissors (no, check that: real scissors, in fact), "lunges at her boss," and then takes the sharpened pair "and turns on herself and cuts one of her wrists."

That's Stevie Smith. Her books were out of print.

She was part of no one's canon.

(Ten years later, Philip Larkin will say that you're not frivolous, that you've been overlooked.)

Was she depressed? (She says she was angry.) Waving? Drowning? Hard to tell the difference. (Had she read Blackmur in the *Kenyon Review*?)

Stevie, I remember you violently. Stevie, I remember you violently. Your scissors are the best part of you.

Teach us to write a poem with scissors, Stevie.

Break, blow, burn. Cut. Heal.

(Remind us a poem remembers what's real.)

PART 2. THE END

John Berryman wanted to bleed.

But there he is, at the end of Blackmur's essay, anointed, canonized, not yet forty. He's helpless as a rich man's child, in a way, child of the Holy Trinity (Pound, Yeats, Eliot). The field's been cleared, the magical scissors are yours, son; the work is "half done" for Berryman, writes Blackmur.

"We might have a great age out of them yet," says the critic inspecting the latest crop. And then he finishes his essay with this slightest touch, and you can feel the self-satisfaction, a mind fat with the glut of hard-won insight. "*What more do you want?*" Poet, what more do you want?

John Berryman wanted to bleed.

Like his dad before him. His last name was Smith, actually. John took his stepdad's. Smith shot his heart out in a Florida dawn.

At least that's one way to view his career arc. From the appointed one of the impersonal modernist creed to the writer of *The Dream Songs*: a search for real scissors he could never quite find. He traveled in the direction of his fear. Disowned Blackmur, felt embarrassed by Eliot, found in Whitman his new father, and concluded, at last, alas, "poetry is composed by actual human beings."

It's a good thing to realize.

But John didn't always know where to find them. Actual human beings.

Turned to minstrelsy, magical voices, bloodless, bodiless, other people's pain, their history, their need.

John just wanted to bleed.

Son of a suicide, he, too, would set himself after his father's business in 1972 (from a bridge, Minnesota). A few years earlier, he sets out to explore a different kind of fall, a different kind of tree, a different kind of self (his character, Henry, in blackface, not me, he wrote, Henry is not me) in what he felt was his poetry, not Eliot's, not Blackmur's.

John's. And Henry's.

(But Henry, dear John, belongs to nobody, belongs to himself. But we're getting ahead of the story. A story about scissors, as you might guess; and cutting; and pop; and actual human beings; and *Olio* by Tyehimba Jess, a black and blues folio, testimony and witness that Henry will never be possessed. But we're getting ahead, we're getting ahead.)

Where were we? John just wanting to bleed.

Berryman, in and out of history, feels like he's out of time. Losing his mind. Casts about for forms, a cast, characters, traditions, a kind of nonsense ministry. Language diminishes: God and us. Can it restore? A late poem from the early *Dream Songs*, about sons like Warhol, and those who bear them; about stars that bleed, and books that can't help but hope to rival them; about Henry who "put forth a book":

No harm resulted from this.
Neither the menstruating stars (nor man) was moved
at once.

Are we divine? No, not yet. Let it bleed. And yet the poem is of two minds, or grows into a different poem, a different thing.

1. There is, at the start, very little lyrical temptation. End-stopped lines that open the poem all hint at trepidation, images of the ineffectuality of artistic creation. Poetry makes nothing happen. Not true actually: "Bare dogs drew closer for a second look // and performed their friendly operations there."

   Nature is not "at once" disturbed, seasons come and go. But then again: the stars are "menstruating."

Loss and mortality, yes, but mother is there, reproductive fertility at odds with "Song 1"—we'll come back to this again, and yet again—where beds only "grow" empty. But what is Henry building after all, a something that seems to be resisting the turn of time and falling leaves. Is it, and this sounds strange, a book or a tree? Whatever it is, it's alive, a living thing. You must admit there's

Something remarkable about this
unshedding bulky bole-proud blue-green moist

thing

2. And what do we make of it, this book/tree, this natural issue he "put forth," with its pages/leaves smelling faintly (don't they?) of canine micturition ("Refreshed, the bark rejoiced"), but aspiring to nothing less than Biblical proportions?

   so that sore on their shoulders old men hoisted
   six-foot sons and polished women called
   small girls to dream awhile toward the flashing
   & bursting tree

   That from which you fall—that upon which you're nailed (let's say)—or is it that which burns and sustains as you approach barefooted?

It's Henry's book, true, Berryman's poems: the new tree—paper upon which we write INRI. I'm nailed right in, says Donne's God after we turn the screws. (Or I'm Not Really Into . . . Who? What? *This life*. Did God have a safe word? Say when? When? At the end of time.)

But it's not just a cross—is it? It's not perfect, no doubt, but it is "unshedding." Fall's not here. We can hope for the best in our ungainly, swollen-tongued sort of way: say "unshedding bulky bole-proud blue-green moist" five times fast.

True. Look at those end-stops disappear. Poetry is capable of something, isn't it? It can "strike the passers from despair" by naming their despair, teaches them to "dream" so as to remember what they have forgotten.

Mark in this tree, and mark in this, Donne might say.

Love and sacrifice. Old men hoist "six-foot" sons on their shoulders.

This song is perhaps the most important in all of *The Dream Songs* because Berryman accepts and reconciles himself to limits—to loss, the little art can do, which is a lot.

This is the all that Joyce's Bloom journeys home for, the word that holds and contains the love and the loss—the pain.

Donne's God is there, Warhol's mother, too.

Actual human beings: in the end, in the end. Then you go back and you begin again.

Part 3: The Beginning

Dreaming of higher places (like Humpty Dumpty), we can begin (now we know how it will end). We read of Huffy Henry who would not face the day; whether he's hiding, or hiding it (the day, when what happened, exactly?), it's hard at first to say. It's a poem, one might say, of careful camouflage, confidences, and confidence men. Who's speaking after all?

> *I see his point,—a trying to put things over.*
> *It was the thought that they thought*
> *they could* do *it made Henry wicked & away.*

Tips on reading when you know the end:

1. "I" can camouflage a poem, can't it? Chatty comments about Henry ("I see his point"; "I don't see how") function to preface what will be Henry's own poem: "a long / wonder the world can bear & be."
2. Where does Henry's poem begin, and the poem about Henry end? These early questions all point to one thing: *The Dream Songs* is a song, sure, but it's more talked about than sung, it's a warm up, a growth, a growing pain. But who sings? It's hard not to think of Blackmur. The new generation of poets, spoiled with the riches of the modern achievement (Pound, Yeats, Eliot), are now "nearer" to song, says the critic.

> *Once in a sycamore I was glad*
> *all at the top, and I sang.*

Are they nearer? Or did they fall? The anxiety of affluence. And who are you, speaking the poem (yeah, you), now a mere character (one of many here), gossipy and vague about poor Henry's life: "It was the thought that they thought / they could *do* it made Henry wicked & away."

You sound horrible, spilling the beans on Henry, don't you? For kicks: Find online a place where Berryman reads this part of the poem. Done in baby voice, because that's what you are—remember, by the end of this book, you'll be lifted on parents' arms, to look, to see.

Like John the Baptist, you must decrease that the other I may increase. Make way for the Lord. Make way! "What he now has to say . . ."

Are you capable of poetry? Are you an actual human being? Or will you steal another's song? Use their done wrongs? So begins the oddly faceless, faithless long poem that will end in flashing and bursting and blood.

Part 4: Poems and Paper Cuts

Stephen Spender, in *The Struggle of the Modern* (written at the time of Berryman's songs), famously depicted the self or "I" as "a conductor between the external terror of modern history and his utterly exposed consciousness to forces he cannot control. . . . A crumbling breakwater against a stormy shore."

Conductor? Music? An orchestral score to shore against our ruin?

Berryman chooses an epigraph from the Book of Lamentations, "I am their Musick." It's the Biblical poet's personal response to general disaster: God (a parent) apparently deserts his people. Not merely, then, "conductor": conscience, consciousness for those who won't let God in. The poet is in dialogue with hate, even, especially that. Venom. Is that it, what Berryman wanted through his "vaudeville turn"?

Let's try that a different way, but now with a full sense of the word conductor in play. The prophet of Lamentations describes the position most clearly when he writes, "I was a derision to all my people; and their song all the day." The litany of curses, the suffering repeated becomes something new. Muse-sick.

The result: a kind of pop duet. Poet defaced, derided, scorned; poet restored, poet reborn, making way for the Lord. Such is the genius, it turns out, not of Berryman, but of Tyehimba Jess, who creates, like Warhol, more or less, scissors in hand, cutting, reconstructing, conducting to exert a new control. Recovering minstrelsy means recovering history, means saying to Berryman: Move over, wounded surgeon. Jess lets us apply the steel (scissors). Poetry as surgery. Cut here. Cut here.

Cut Here -------------------- -----------------: Olio

Jess in *Olio,* which won the Pulitzer Prize for poetry in 2017, performs this surgery, reminds me that Henry is not Berryman's, "can't tell my tale at all," but a man in time, living, breathing, one whom no one could possess (Henry "Box" Brown, a slave, mailed himself to freedom, to Philly, to deliverance. In a box.)

Liberate him from Berryman's pages, says Jess, "let Box Henry grow in every head," reusing, refusing "Song 1," now a fertility wish for a culture where no longer "empty grows every bed." It's a wish for a truly popular culture, a historical consciousness. This is a "Freedsong." Free Henry. Free the poem. Turn to the page you can detach ("let your scissors rend paper to illuminate this argument"). Let Henry clap back, even duet with the slave catcher. Audience, clap, clap back. Cut. Deep cuts. What is pop, if not that?

These are endmen. One seeks to end the other. The other, Henry, boxed in, is just beginning: "I declare salvation of myself." Behold, call and response. Poetry double-faced, like Lamentations, facing off, Yaweh to the left of me, haters to the right. This is song. This is equipment for living: "He thought he could *do* it," Jess makes us rethink—

Berryman, what he could not do.

Makes us think, too, of how a song is not just a voice thrown, a cover, a put on. It's a kind of box, a space, a room, a place to hide, survive, "made well, / unlike us," with air to breathe, escape, be free. I was cautioned to surrender, says "Box Henry," like Leonard Cohen's Partisan: I chose instead this bid for freedom, this livable design.

Jess's book is that box, a box of songs. It lets you stretch in sonnets, little rooms. You read from top to bottom or bottom up. Sideways, too. Sturdy songs. Use your scissors: You're free to do that, too. As one reviewer puts it, "Much of *Olio* must be read and re-read: the final pages provide origami-like instructions that reveal new imagery and understandings previously hidden in the poem's original structure." Origami, like a haiku, is a way to do a lot with a little—cuts, lines, words. Just a few.

Indeed, a poem should curve, Joel Dias-Porter (DJ Renegade) once taught me, and he reminds me here again (he consulted on some of *Olio*'s visual ideas, I've heard).

Scissors. Real scissors. Cut the chord. And this is how we heal. Pop. Returned to people, reclaimed, remembered, restored, renewed. Scissors and poems remember what's real.

This is homage. This is pop elegy, what art can give.

A seven-year-old cuts a movie idol from a mag. Mom cuts flowers from cans. You can. Live.

John needs to bleed, but art, real art, wants something more.

Every day: a page, a poet, a word, a people previously hidden now transformed. Traditions unmasked. Every day. Every day. Every day.

Henry is not me. He's been cut. He's been torn. Henry is not me. Henry is reborn.

Part 5: God Cuts Leonard Loose

Leonard, you're dying, although not yet. Still you want to write a love song.

Why do I think of you?

"Going Home," a late Cohen song, returns us to Lamentations and to God in a way that reframes all of this, much like Jess; does what Berryman wanted to do all along, "come out and talk," with God, through God, about God, and about us. God, of course, wants Leonard to cut it out. But poets never listen. That's why Cohen reminds me of a kind of redeemed Berryman, a poet who does not jump from the Washington Avenue Bridge in the winter of 1972 and into the Mississippi below, a poet who knows that the minor fall may very well be followed by the major lift.

His plane lifts off for a world tour as Berryman's brightness falls through the air, a tour that'll give us *Live Songs* in 1974, songs like journeys, like journeyman's songs, most but not all his own, like "Passing Through," a lazy anthem, about leisure, and pleasure, and passing time, and running into people like Jesus and Adam. Chatty, which in Cohen's world means that it's serious, the logic of Cohen's lyrical dialogic. See Adam leave the garden. Now he's out, what's he going to do?

Plant some crops and pray for rain, maybe raise a little cane.
I'm an orphan now, and I'm only passing through.

In this they're alike, Cohen and Berryman, with their jokes and that feeling of eavesdropping, listening in. "I've heard there was a secret chord," begins "Hallelujah," a rumor of a king, and we spy David spying on Bathsheba over the eaves. Salvation is a rumor to gossip about. Back-and-forth patter ("you don't really care for music, do ya?") makes you feel presence. Someone's talking to ya.

In late Cohen there's a stripping down, not Bathsheba stripping for her bath, but rather the young woman stripping her clothes in monastic retreat (the video for the single "Happens to the Heart" off the posthumous *Thanks for the Dance*). Cohen is going home. It's time to do what you're told, what God tells you to do. To cut it out. Can you? Will you? "I was always working steady / But I never called it art." Late Cohen is about God, and what God wants from your heart. Don't call it art.

A song about choruses and burdens, about making something strong. "Going Home" is about repeating rather than making something new. It's a song about Leonard, an actual human being, from God's point of view.

I love to speak with Leonard
He's a sportsman and a shepherd
He's a lazy bastard
Living in a suit

Not Henry but Leonard, lazy as Jacob perhaps but perhaps as wily, too. With his own agenda, a few tricks up his Armani sleeve. God loves to speak to him, and through him ("But he does say what I tell him"), because, being a poet, he's boxed in.

He just doesn't have the freedom
To refuse

Cohen's songs tell us we're not all that free. When the frontiers are your prison, you do what you're told. There's a measure to things and especially songs, and the stakes are too high for getting them wrong. At least God thinks so.

He will speak these words of wisdom
Like a sage, a man of vision

Then, of course, comes the burden, the shared refrain, which God lets his poet have. At least that, if nothing else. Because, before long, Leonard won't have anything.

Going home
Without my burden
Going home
Behind the curtain

What we want to conduct and what we must conduct—what God wants—is the tension here. God wants, too; as Adam and Eve knew, hiding in the Garden, God wants to be loved. Which is of course nothing (nothing?) but a kind of effacement of will, sacrificed on an altar where there is no want, no desire. Of course, as Cohen admits, there may also be no more poetry, which means this late song is a kind of farewell to conducting, to singing, to the anthems and the cries that made Leonard Leonard.

God looks on. Sees his suffering servant who wants to do so many things, write so many things, wants, wants, wants 1) to write "a love song" 2) "an anthem of forgiving" 3) "a manual for living with defeat" 4) "a cry above the suffering" 5) "a sacrifice recovering," but Leonard, says God, no.

That isn't what I need him
To complete

What does God want?

In a word, us, all to himself, like a jealous lover; or perhaps, better, to be us, for Leonard to return to him, his image and likeness, relieving him of the recon mission we call this life, this passing through.

I want him to be certain
That he doesn't have a burden

But we do.

God knows this, of course, so the poet's asked

To say what I have told him
To repeat

Repeat. Repeat. What we do with burdens. How we share, and in sharing alleviate the suffering. Of course, Leonard's most famous burden, his Hallelujah, did just that, a repetition of a king, king of kings, repeated by you, and you, and Jeff Buckley, too. But his songs tell us what Berryman never knew. The poet-conductor doesn't need his own vision, or anyone's at all. Songs are a measure of surrender. You live in that space and there you are free.

Late Cohen is the pleasure of surrender, the feeling that art has been immolated, and what's left are just bones, the shape of things, the burdens we share. What's left is not the self and its wants, but the forms we follow, placing our trust that the master knows where we're going. One foot in front of another. Don't call it art, says Cohen at the end: "It was just some old convention / Like the horse before the cart."

But this late song, "Going Home," courting death, says something else as well. About God, lonely God who loves to speak with his servant. God wants to be loved, as Donne realized. Loving him is easy, the burden is light, so to speak, because we must simply repeat, and in reproducing affirm this love.

Yes, I said, yes, says Molly Bloom.

Yes, yes, y'all. Yes, yes, y'all. Did we ever wonder what we're saying yes to?

All.

Yes, yes, y'all.

Keep on, Leonard, till the break of dawn. Keep on. Till the break of dawn. Don't call it art. I won't call it art. Keep on. Keep on. Till the break of dawn.

For that is when lovers must part.

3
A Photograph of a Little Room

Philip Larkin's Selfie

There's a picture of Philip Larkin you've probably never seen. He's youngish, but it's always hard to tell with Larkin, endlessly balding, bespectacled Larkin the librarian, stranded in the north of England, bloating like a frog. He cultivated that myth, of course, that bow-tied, buttoned-up vision of himself standing athwart the times that are a-changin'.

Needless to say, he hated Bob Dylan, Charlie Parker, and, yes, there's the bow tie, nearly at the center of all that sepia.

He's thin here, alone, taking a picture of a mirror, which of course is what we all did before our phones grew smarter. He includes what he doesn't have to, too, jacket on a jacket hook, a bottle cap that turns to two, clutter, bric-a-brac before the mirror.

Larkin, Kardashian.

No. I think of snow in a Pictorialist dream, a quiet, blurred city from long ago. Was that even true? Things change. Maybe they don't. Can a form be *selfish*? And what's that even mean? What are forms but rooms you put yourself in, self-portraits that keep things out, let things in?

Larkin wants to find out. Maybe he is taking a picture of a room that holds his reflection, not him, not the poet. The distinction is worth making. After all, this is the poet who would write,

Such attics cleared of me! Such absences!

Of course, Larkin doesn't really want absence. The "nothing . . . nowhere" is what most terrified him. He sought form, shape, order, like Andy dreaming of becoming a pop artist, dreaming of his mother's pantry.

He found it, here, in the camera, which he bends over like a sprinter at the block, dedicated, serious, reproducing the self in its little cell, its little room, spare, orderly but not, like a kitchen.

Larkin found this extension of the self, this ordering of the self, in another little room—the sonnet form—with its voltas that turn like a hinge and couplets that close like a door. A selfish form, in his hands, like a camera in his room, like a picture of a room with a man inside.

How artists use forms—techniques of reproduction, repetition, structure—to imagine themselves, to reproduce themselves in the world is what we see when we look at the librarian, like we saw in the ad-man, the suicide. Like Warhol, they ask us to think about the power of reproduction—the power of art—and how it pictures us in the world. Not alone but connected to others.

A Sonnet in a Bombed-Out Church

On Philip Larkin
(feat. Stevie Smith and Charlie Parker)

Part 1. Aubade in Handcuffs

Your body is a cage.

It keeps you from the one you love. Or maybe I'm thinking of time, of all that time will do to you.

Dreamers wake in the dark and drown (with time to think this can't be true).

Alba! Sunrise!

Aubade: obey. It's a poem of parting lovers: the aubade. Morning's here. Watchman calls. Tells us what we always knew. Know. One of us will have to go.

It's time; time's the cage we must—can't—slip. Rise and shine, Ezra Pound, did you sleep well on the cold Italian ground? Did you dream of "Alba," an aubade you once did write? Translator still translating inside his little cage, 1945, enemy of the state. "Their look translated to me as 'gorilla, stay in your cage!'" (Translators can't help but translate.)

Time holds you in its chains. That's what the aubade says. But poets resist. Build a little room, draw the curtains, hide in a body for at least a little while. Still, light gets in: time, desire. Turns out, a poem is a safe space (and not). Time's a vampire. Vampire weekend. Rostam sees the light coming through: "I knew it / But can't see it, I refuse." In John Donne's aubade, there's the sun, its rising, its rays:

I could eclipse and cloud them with a wink,
But that I would not lose her sight so long

Your body is a cage, but it's also a room. That's what the poem builds on the page, what the aubade shows the contours of. Morning hardens upon the wall (Thomas Hardy), and the violence of your desire—to live, what else?—becomes plain, plain, Philip Larkin writes in "Aubade," "as a wardrobe" (or maybe a pantry). Look, his poem says: "The room takes shape."

Time brings death and time brings light and light brings form and forms endure (even if we don't). Wait for it. Wait for it: the light. And in that waiting repeat, delay, which is maybe just another way to say, create. Play. Imagine the form of another day.

The poem, then, is a room, but it's torn, a divided house. Here's torrin a. greathouse. Their work in *Poetry* a litany of spaces, rooms, and cells designed sometimes by the self, sometimes by others: "How many lovers," greathouse writes in "Aubade Beginning in Handcuffs,"

> *have said that*
> *they adore me, but meant instead they saw*
> *in me a door? A thing to be entered. Language*

Reminding us of Donne, of Donne's play with the sun, greathouse pays homage to the aubade's desire. To be one and more than one. To stay; to be contained. Donne: "All here in one bed lay."

To be all.

Dreamers wake in the dark and drown, with time to think this can't be true. (Frederick Seidel, unsuicidal, greets the dawn in a three-piece suit.)

Larkin, writing about his ending, begins his aubade at the high point of his career, 1974, but can't quite finish it. That year *High Windows* marks a height he will never again reach.

Writing about rooms his entire life, he once more tries, after his mother dies. There is a crack; here comes the light. November 1977. Soon after he gets it right.

(He was trying his entire life.)

Part 2. Philip Larkin Was a Teenager

It's hard to believe, I know.

What do we know about the poet who was rated England's most popular in the twentieth century and turned down the Laureate like he was Johnny Rotten? He had "a sense of humor that has aged badly," James Fenton puts it mildly. If there is a keyword for the poet's posthumous career, "reactionary" certainly fits the bill—the new Completes fill out the profile of someone whose professed goal in arranging the *Oxford Book of Twentieth-Century English Verse* was to make the war-torn age's poetry "sound nice."

Strange, then, for such a backward-looking poet that critics have been slow to look back: Where did he come from? From there, where did he go? Or did he stay, more or less, in the same room, the same poem, with the sun breaking the branches to get through the window?

Philip ♥ Stevie

Philip & Stevie, sitting in a tree, W-I-S-H-I-N-G they were somewhere, anywhere else.

Philip Larkin, teenager, bespectacled, slightly balding youth haunting the school grounds: I think of you thinking of Stevie Smith and her scissors (scissors she used in anger, or was it to make something new?). Something in the older poet appealed to you. What was it? Just another Smith among Smiths in England, true, hemmed in like a boar between arches, but she spoke to you, the librarian who passed out her books as Christmas gifts. Your bemused friends.

Philip, they said, this is stupid stuff.

Both of you stayed at home, building rooms in your poems, poems in your rooms.

"Frivolous and Vulnerable," the name of the review Larkin published in 1962 on Smith, tried to show she was really neither. It worked, and didn't. "Frivolous" and eccentric would long be connected with her name after that review. Childish and superficial, too. Smith, who illustrated her poems with drawings, cartoons; who draws, who scratches the surface, like Leopold Bloom writing on the sand with a stick: "I AM A." "Feminine doodler,'" Larkin called her, one "who puts down everything as it strikes her." He wrote that and not without approval.

Behold the doodler, like Eimear McBride's child playing around with red pens, cutting Jesus, Heaney, history in *A Girl Is a Half-Formed Thing*. Like Bloom on the toilet, jotting down Molly's words on his cuff. Off the cuff, playing, doodling, larking about.

"Poor chap, he always loved larking," says (who, exactly?)—you, reader, you—in Smith's most famous poem, "Not Waving but Drowning." The dead man is now dead as the poem ends. Why? What killed him? You did. No one had read him closely enough. The swimmer who was telling you he could not swim.

Of course, rarely is larking taken seriously. Why would it be? And why should early Larkin—dead man larking—even ever be read?

What was Larkin doing, exactly, in his late teenage years?

Starting his aubade, for one thing, which would take him another fifty years; and that meant skipping prom to master the sonnet, which meant learning about time and the handcuffs of form, how things rhyme (and can't or won't or do, like the door of a prison cell closing shut). His apprentice years were spent scissoring, like Stevie Smith, Julia Warhola, through intractable stuff—tradition, the sonnet form.

Though you wouldn't know it. And with good reason: Larkin of the 1940s and 1950s, according to Fenton, confirms for us what we always already knew: "English poems of this period not seldom chucked in a unicorn when all else failed." Did everyone know? About the unicorns?

This myth, of course, was Larkin's own; immature, "isolated," and "in search for a style" is how he wrote about himself in a preface to the 1966 reissue of *The North Ship* (1945), calling himself in a letter written as an eighteen-year-old, "not the truly strong man but . . . a *Peg's Paper* sonneteer."

Peg's Paper was a British women's magazine (1920–1940) that published romance fiction for working class girls of the era. Pulp, pop: the stuff of "feminine doodlers," perhaps, which Larkin would do in fiction form, too, under the name Brunette Coleman. Odd to think of sonnets as pulpy, as doodling and pop—somehow needing to be dismissed, repressed. But that's just what Larkin did, excluding them from his slim published work.

Why?

Written while balding Philip was also Brunette—was there something "vulnerable," like Smith's work, that also fascinated him, disquieted him, too?

What did the form teach him? And us?

And what's it mean to read the form—a sonnet; it's really nothing much—as a kind of doodling, a rehearsing and reusing?

Larkin, who hated Charlie Parker for what he did to jazz.

But it's what you did, Philip, too. I won't say tables are turned, because turntables are scratched, remixed. That's not you. But things get demolished, and you show us how to save the old by making it new.

There is a line of Smith's that Larkin set aside for emphasis: "I shall be glad to be silent, Mother, and hear you speak." There's childish gravity there: reticence and attention of child and mother, like Andy and Julia. Call it the lyric voice in remission; or call it tradition; or call it, why not?, the mom in pop.

Larkin called it "an authority of sadness" that defined Smith's work. The Pope of Mope, the Hermit of Hull. Yes, Larkin was all that, and much more (or much worse). But he was also, like Smith, a child listening to mother, a teenage doodler in a wasteland (Coventry) where he says his childhood was "unspent," undoing forms like bombs undoing churches, leaving us to wonder, *what it all ever meant?*

Bombs?

Violence: Or, a Bomb in a Church

November 14, 1940. Here's the church, and here's the steeple. Here's Coventry's medieval cathedral. See the Luftwaffe drop the bombs; see them fall on top of the people. Or as an eyewitness told the BBC, a mere fourteen-year-old girl (and maybe a female doodler, who put everything down as it struck her): "I saw a dog running down the street with a child's arm in its mouth. There were lines of bodies stretched out on blankets."

Lines of poetry, lines of bodies. These are modern forms, adding up to what? Things blow up. Things blow up, that's what. How do you contain them? How do you even begin to try? I guess what I'm trying to say is this: What do you do with all these lines?

Isn't that the question of pop, and the question of poetry? We organize our pantry. Home edit. Maybe it's art. But is it all just a way to save a world we know will fall apart?

I write these lines, Larkin, in 2019. I'm in a café in Genoa. There is no lockdown. Nothing is viral. A tourist, I tour the Italian city's famous cathedral, *Duomo di Genova, Cattedrale di San Lorenzo,* and say a prayer to a bomb that stands unexploded there. The British Navy delivered it here three months after Coventry was broken, blown up, and burned. The bomb tore open a wall in the cathedral but did not explode.

Call it a miracle. People do. Quiet it stands like a saint in its niche, stands like a sentinel.

Tonight we hear music. A band covers Pearl Jam and Italians sing along and we do, too. Things change by not changing at all, sings Eddie Vedder, and though he's singing about a woman behind a counter, like a painting by Hopper, I think of forms and how they're not their former; and for the first time in a long time that I can remember, I think about how a song is like a bomb that is still a bomb and not a bomb at all. (It's a miracle.) It's shaped like the roof of a church, or the shape of your hands forming a steeple. Your daughter. She looks inside her hands and tells you she's praying and—look!—there are the people. And at once you remember Amiri Baraka's "Preface to a Twenty Volume Suicide Note," when he sees his daughter "on her knees, peeking into / Her own clasped hands," and you know for certain, without a doubt, you know for certain the poet was thinking of his daughter and churches and bombs which have nothing to do with each other except, of course, they do.

"Young girl, violence." I always thought Eddie Vedder sang *violins.* Things change. Or we do.

I pray to the unexploded bomb in the Genoa cathedral because it's a miracle, because it's a form for measuring time like a sonnet; and it lets time do what time does to every form, which is simply this: It makes forms legible. That's what happens to forms over time: Change by not changing at all. You read them and read them again and they are not as they were and you are not as you were. All things become new and possible. A sonnet. A bomb. A bomb in a cathedral.

Make it new! says Ezra Pound, repeating the Shang dynasty's first king (1766–1753 BC). Things change by not changing. A modernist manifesto; a slogan on the washbasin of a king.

But here's the thing. When I think of Larkin at eighteen writing sonnets while a city explodes and the dog makes off with the child's arm in its mouth and the bodies are lined up and history will not turn, will not turn like a volta, and will not end like a sonnet with the comfort of a couplet, I think of a poet practicing an elegy for form's failure; I think of a balding young man who will call himself Brunette writing a song of loss for what art cannot save, cannot protect (and maybe never could), no matter its dream, no matter the glory it entertained; I think of him looking up at high windows (which used to be there) and looking higher and even higher; and all that I mean is that I think of poetry of endurance and failure, endurance and failure; that poets build little rooms in houses on fire: not to show you how everything burns but to show you instead the shape of the fire.

Part 3. A Sonnet Is a Little Room

Like the dream of his selfie, Larkin was most proud of poems very different from his sonnets. He favored post-symbolist works like his "Absences" that emptied out the self—depictions "of what places look like when I am not there"—and poems like "High Windows" that show "the beauty of somewhere you're not." O, to be anywhere else, to be anyone else, thinks every emo-teenage-sonneteer, thinks everyone, everywhere.

Though Larkin found himself decidedly, inescapably penned in by the sonnet, he never forgot his schooling in the form. It's where he first meditated on the problem of being a self, a self that is always somewhere.

If "the little room of the sonnet serves as an echo chamber and amplifier," as Adam Kirsch puts it, for Larkin it is most often a waiting room, where the speaker finds himself in conflict. With time. With the stinging awareness of being human. Human limits.

Forms for Larkin are like Christian Marclay's *The Clock*; they quite literally—often painfully—measure it all. Time, the light breaking through. Like Rostam's *Half-Light*, Larkin's at his best in bedroom poems like "Aubade" and "Sad Steps," where he refuses to look at the light (but then doesn't refuse). Old man poems came to him, more or less, as a teenager; that's what's so strange. Perhaps he was bemused, and that's surely not the right word, by his body (a cage), his country (a cage), and his family (ditto). By all small, frustrated romances (very small 'r,' fitting the *Peg's Paper* sonneteer). "Why aren't they screaming?" Larkin asked about the elderly in his fifties. But the question was a selfie of sorts for the poet long before, a ringing in the ears, an echo in his sonnets.

Take, for example, the unpublished "Autobiography at an Air-Station" (1953), a summary of his apprentice years. Airports may be painful to someone who lived through the 1940s, but not here. Here is modern deliverance, its threat and promise, which is just another way to say, in Larkin's world: Behold, the dream of bureaucracy.

"Autobiography" reminds us (and it's easy to forget) the sonnet was "the first lyric form since the fall of the Roman Empire intended not for music or performance but for silent reading. As such, it is the first lyric of self-consciousness, or of the self in conflict." That's Paul Oppenheimer in *The Birth of the Modern Mind.* And here's Larkin at the airport doodling, which is to say putting down everything as it strikes him: "We sit in steel chairs, buy cigarettes and sweets."

Like the newspapers the travelers "unfold" while waiting for their flight, the sonnet is, for Larkin, just one more piece of isolated reading. It's your phone and feeling like you're feeding with your finger. Leading nowhere. But not quite. You scroll. Larkin scrolls. But the sonnet is different, a form for mapping a modern logic onto the page, a place to doodle, to trace geometries: its coordinates the lines of people, repetition, incomprehensibility, and, of course, quiet rage.

What makes the poem feel so true is this: It's not a realization one makes over time, a kind of fall into knowledge and sin. Rather, for Larkin, and you might agree, it's just how things begin. Look around. It's hard to get started, to begin.

Delay, well, travelers must expect
Delay. For how long? No one seems to know.

Curiously impersonal, like being addressed by Alexa, your echo—No "I" is present here. You're a traveler, you're at their (whose?) mercy, and, please, try not to make a fuss. There's a way of doing things, you guess (though no one seems to really know).

The English sonnet is a way of doing things. It becomes proxy for safety and a semblance of order that always in Larkin unravels. "We" gives way soon enough, questions pile up, and delaying caesuras of each line finally hit a roadblock "No" in line seven right at the sonnet's turn. "Ought we to smile, / Perhaps make friends?"

No: in the race for seats
You're best alone. Friendship is not worth while.

Sonnets of the air are not such rare birds. There's W. B. Yeats's "Leda and the Swan." Like Yeats, Larkin opts for an Italian sestet (efg/efg) to advance the second part in a poem where no one goes anywhere at all. It's how you make things fall apart, in a way, or do what bombs do by undoing what we think can't be undone. From English to Italian form, Larkin plays with forms, to unspool, disrupt, and scramble. What, exactly? Hope for progress: for comfort, closure, the couplet. Lines of words, lines of bodies that might go somewhere turn instead into dimmer and dimmer versions of themselves, echoes like a stepping into sleep, into darkness, into night. Couple(t)s get erased, grow distant, paler. "The thousands of marriages," writes Larkin elsewhere, "lasting a little while longer."

What do you do in the face of this?

Delay, delay. That is the name of the modern game after all. The machine breaks down. Delay. Monkeydoodles the whole thing. Delay. Repetition as endlessness, as alienation. But the morning is coming, light is breaking. And now you want delay. It's rooted in our desire. It's a pop calculus, this play, how you beat them at their own game. Doodle, dawdle. Stretch things out. Art makes nothing happen, but can it at least help you save your life? Is that too much to ask? Perhaps. But you can give it a shot.

Just a quick thought: What's it mean to delay when you know you can't make anything stop? No one seems to know how, seems to know anything at all. But still we try and in trying try to keep it all at bay. We wait for it. We write in handcuffs. We live that way.

Let's wait for it. The end of "Autobiography." Let's delay getting to its end (and ours). You must know how it ends already. Remember "Aubade": "The room takes shape," another day, another shape to stave off ruin, the end. We'll wait for it.

Teenage Larkin knew this, knew that forms and rituals and routines would never do (but what if that's all we've got?), and so chops up what's been given, like Julia Warhola, turning old things into something new. Forms, it's true, can parody what we think we can get out of them (protection, security) in a world where fire drops from the sky and no one, not one person is safe.

The dog runs down the street and takes the child's arm away.

The little girl sees it all.

Bodies line the street, parody of geometry.

Speaking of geometry, here's the schoolmaster in "Schoolmaster" (1940):

He sighed with relief. He had got the job. He was safe.

A devastating way to begin, with someone knowing nothing, so tenured, so safe, isn't it? This is eighteen-year-old Larkin, doing Auden-like cadences in different voices. Unchanging, confident, triadic: a line that changes by not wanting to change at all. What's it mean to write sonnets, after all, to relish safety and complacency in a time of war? What do we mean, really, when we rely on forms?

The job, form, routine will surely work its magic, we're told, to "ma[k]e him a god." It's a dream vision of sorts in "Schoolmaster," clock time silenced, years turning into "aisles of stone," unlike the cathedral's that can and will get blown to bits.

Yes, of course, the possibility of failure makes its appearance at the volta in the voice of "Others" who challenge the Schoolmaster with "the claims of living." Groan. "They were merely desperate." These sonnets are inviolable, selfish spaces, like the self itself, like a book of pure Kardashian.

The poems conspire with you; make you feel confident, which means terrified—because you know, don't you? Just like in "Autobiography," nothing happens, which is what's most terrifying. No bombs go off. No sudden realization. No apparition at the train station. Lacking real connection—the purview, once upon a time, of the sonnet—the self simply dissolves.

And so does the sonnet, a form turning into a shadow of a form. A flaccid final couplet tries to remind you, do you remember?, this was a sonnet after all. Do you remember?

For though he never realized it, he
Dissolved. (Like sugar in a cup of tea).

Parenthetical endings like this indict. They are a proving ground of sorts for the kind of weaponry an older Larkin called the "successful conclusion." He was thinking, oddly, about Emily Dickinson: "Only rarely, however, did she bring a poem to successful conclusion . . . too often the poem expires in a teased-out and breathless obscurity." Larkin wanted to be the strong man. He wanted precision engineering, and, ironically (or maybe not so), that's what he practiced in these schoolboy exercises, writing his schoolgirl fiction, and his schoolbook sonnets, like once upon a time when school kids twirled batons.

What Goes Up: On Twirling Batons and Burning Homes

What was it all for? Those forms? Those turns? Exercises and practices? You sat down at the piano, and what did you learn? Is this tradition? Must it always seem so absurd?

Thinking of Larkin, I think of a young Sissy Spacek, which, yes, is odd, I think, but maybe not so. Can you see her practicing pivots at the start of Terrence Malick's *Badlands* (1973)?

Do you remember Holly, strawberry blonde, twirling her baton, freckles, one-step-two-step-and-then-a-big-toss? Watch the twirling baton, and the mind reels in light of the aimless murder to follow, her knock-off James Dean beau, Kit Carruthers (Martin Sheen), a parody of forms, a parody of characters, a couple of kids playacting a bankrupt tradition. They set her house on fire, one of the great sequences of 1970s cinema, released about the time of *High Windows.* Watch it burn. Watch the dollhouse burn. Violence. Malick cues the violins. You search for forms. For Julia Warhola's wedding album. Her scorched home. "Home is so sad. It stays as it was left," Larkin writes at the start of the 1960s. Well, not always. Not always. A parody of a home; Holly's voice-over narration a parody of narration, even. No wonder it's been so influential.

Such was the fate of forms in the late twentieth century, rehearsed in the pop culture, but also redeemed there, too. Like Larkin's voltas that turn and pivot like a girl twirling a baton, these forms gives us no relief; the baton will fall, bodies will fall, and the music plays as a father's body burns. Larkin's final couplets, too, burn, turn: to ashes. They dissolve into stray lines, existential addendums, afterthoughts.

But he forgot all this as he grew older.

So ends a sonnet written by the nineteen-year-old poet, not much older than Holly. "Older" rhymes with "wonder," of course, something you used to do (didn't you?) when you were younger. Perhaps you don't remember the rhyme because it came so many lines (years) before. You're older than that now. And think you speak with authority. Or maybe it's the parody of authority. Like everyone else (surely someone must know). Like Holly recounting her travels. Missing the forest for the trees. Lose your illusion. You're supposed to.

Larkin's is a poetry of dissolution, disillusion.

But in the meantime the baton twirls in the air. This is also a poetics of delay, hands moving on the clock, and maybe, just maybe a bit of play: "I can't deny we've had fun though," says mass murderer Kit Carruthers, recording a fake suicide note (a minute for fifty cents) at a gramophone booth. He's buying time. Well, no murder in Larkin. This is a poetry of killing time, in every sense of the word. Of course, that's what art does. Here comes the morning, and another day. The sonnet, in Larkin's hand, becomes an app for measuring that: anticipating, remembering, dreading, forgetting. Ignoring. Is there a better definition of art? It's a way of enduring.

Now you remember, or did you forget?, Larkin's "Autobiography at an Air Station," the race for seats, the looking ahead to your own transcendence, your flight, the god-machine that will ravish you, salvage you, transform you, the modern form that snatches you up like a swan?

Well, no such luck.

Here's the volta, the sonnet's turn into, what else?, time and what ifs.

Six hours pass: If I'd gone by boat last night
I'd be there by now. Well, it's too late for that.

We're brought with the sestet into the sixth hour of delay; six lines are left, and you're at sixes (and then at sevens). We are in real time here, not unlike waking at 4 a.m. in "Sad Steps" in line four of the poem ("Four o'clock: wedge-shadowed gardens lie / Under a cavernous, a wind-picked sky").

Aubade: obey. Time is a cage, and this preoccupies Larkin from his teen years to his final "Aubade," half a century, the idea of time and form, art as a system of deliverables that never quite does deliver. But it tries. Endures. Measures. Waits for. We wait for what, precisely?

Darkness swarms; travelers yawn; the doodling poet, feeling "staled," will repeat the theme of time's chains that hold him fast for the rest of his career:

I set
So much on this Assumption. Now it's failed.

Jet set. Not yet. Never, in fact. No comfort in the couplet here; no couplet at all; no comfort in mother (the Virgin, we assume); and no future, no promise—not even the assumption of Assumption. The poet must face "now," writing his aubade in handcuffs. It's tough but it's not teased-out. It's a burning house. The house is on fire, or maybe that's just the way the sunrise hits the window. It's a powerful conclusion in "Autobiography," no doubt, like Smith's own famous ending for her most famous poem, "I was much too far out all my life / And not waving but drowning." Maybe Larkin was onto something in his criticism of Dickinson and how she ended her poems, but only if we give him the benefit of the doubt. Form, that limited resource, is all he's got, he thought. If you're stuck in a cell, well, at least you want to hear the door slam shut.

His critical writing, mostly, is a fight for handcuffs, for formal bonds that bind us together in mutual survival and struggle. He's against those who are against that. It's why he elegizes (the past? churches? belief?) in "Church Going," and why you feel a sonnet haunting "Sad Steps," which takes, it turns out, its title from a sonnet by Sidney.

Though he'd soon leave the sonnet behind, too practiced in its deflations and counterpoints, it's where he learned to measure time, lighten its weight, and wait for the light. And one lesson was this (and it was an important one): Endings don't so much sting as they stun. Beginnings, too. No comfort. No quarter. To live is to struggle is to endure. This is pop. A pop sensibility. It fucks you up. Do I have your attention?

May I have your attention, please?

Yes, Slim Shady, please stand up. My attention is yours.

This is pop. It fucks you up. Fucks you up, the mom in pop.

For Larkin, this be the truth, this be the Bible, chapter, verse. The fucking goes all the way through, from start to finish: it's like a curse.

But that's not all. You follow its curve like a tulip or a gun. The poem has a shape to it; that's what lets you get a grip. You can feel it. You can hold on tight. You won't slip.

Now, behold, darkness is gone. The rising of the sun.

Now, as "Aubade" reveals in the breaking of the light, "Work has to be done."

Part 4. Charlie Parker Had a Daughter

Obscurity was Larkin's battle cry against modernism writ large, the "Picasso, Parker, Pound" effect that dissolved the bond between artist and audience in a fog of abstraction. Or so he thought. With his early schooling in the sonnet in mind, Larkin's remarks read more like a history of how traditional, communal forms were mishandled, ignored. The cathedral breached in the time of war.

> *It seems to me undeniable that up to this century literature used language in the way we all use it, painting represented what anyone with normal vision sees, and music was an affair of nice noises rather than nasty ones.*

So goes a *Paris Review* interview with the poet who wanted to make the age's poetry "sound nice." Larkin's acidity is pretty well known, but it reads rather differently, I think, when you think of his sonnets and churches exploding and Coventry's population descending into "hysteria, terror, neurosis" overnight. I'm thinking of Larkin thinking of pop's handcuffs, the way measures and forms serve communal functions, bind together nation, lovers, parent and child with everything from anthems to lullabies, not to mention the music of Armstrong and Bechet and Bessie Smith.

Modernism ruined all of that.

Says Larkin.

Like the music of Charlie Parker, *Bird*, who descends like a "paranoiac drug addict" (Larkin's words) flying his plane with sights locked on the imaginary of the librarian's (bald) dome:

> *Charlie Parker wrecked jazz by—or so they tell me—using the chromatic rather than the diatonic scale. The diatonic scale is what you use if you want to write a national*

> *anthem, or a love song, or a lullaby. The chromatic scale is what you use to give the effect of drinking a quinine martini and having an enema simultaneously.*

It's dead now, all dead, Larkin ends, "dead as Elizabethan madrigal singing."

So, Charlie Parker killed the sonnet. Who knew? Paranoia aside on Larkin's part, here's the really interesting part: If Larkin's sonnets reflect this longing for community, they also feature imprisoned, isolated, even paranoid selves—rejecting others, selves that find their flights grounded, the walls of the cathedral blasted, the roof caved in. Larkin's sonnets, in other words, are pulp, pop. Call them bebop. Why not? They are autobiographies of modern selves: birds caged like the Charlie Parker of Larkin's mind.

Larkin both is and isn't a modernist (like every modernist). His mature work in poems like "Sad Steps" is haunted by death, sure, and by dead Elizabethans. This traditional, populist note—for a golden age when we all saw the same things and sang the same songs—is, in a kinder light, a kind of dream of pop, isn't it? A kind of *Bird Box* dream. Maybe it's not as sentimental as it seems. It's a dream not of nostalgia but a collective embrace of dissonance. Of today. Together. We can find a way. Singing from our balconies. Literature in lockdown. *Let us begin.* Let us start. (Look around. We are pop art.)

And yes, of course, The Movement poets (like Larkin and Thom Gunn) would not "abandon a rational structure and comprehensible language," as Robert Conquest put it in his introduction to *New Lines: An Anthology* (1956). But even in his most structured works—his sonnets—Larkin makes clear that no way does he see the same things "as anyone with normal vision sees." He is a different kind of bird altogether. In other words, he shares more in common with Parker than he'd like to admit.

Odd but true, this is the argument of one of his few published sonnets, "Spring," from *The Less Deceived* (1955). It's a neat remix. One of the first sonnets in the English language, "Description of Spring" ("The soote season") by Henry Howard, Earl of Surrey, gets sampled, even the alliterative line of the Anglo-Saxon tradition. And all in a curious way. Surrey's green, surging world feels supercharged. It's got what the Jesuit poet Hopkins calls "juice."

The soote season, that bud and bloom forth brings,
With green hath clad the hill, and eke the vale.
The nightingale with feathers new she sings;
The turtle to her make hath told her tale.

Larkin echoes Surrey's form (even the opening rhyme). But the sweet life is drained: "Green-shadowed people sit, or walk in rings." Strange, to carefully sap the alliteration of its energy, like a teenage Charlie Parker mastering (and calmly reshaping, reusing) jazz history one hothouse summer in the Ozarks. Larkin's green world is "calm," static, arrested, unnatural in its opening allusion to the Waste Landers Eliot saw "walking round in a ring":

Their children finger the awakened grass,
Calmly a cloud stands, calmly a bird sings

Will this bird fly? "Spring" gives us a different Larkin. Not just mourning the fragmented self, this is the vision of the *flâneur*, whose alienation, bird-like, is precisely what enables him to see. See what? Himself, his incompleteness. After all, what else does art ever make us see? Coke-bottle lenses and all. Call it pop vision.

The sonnet solo starts here, and I strongly advise listening to Parker as you read the rest: the lines riff on, well, not so much individuality, as on a vision, simply, of "me." Me is a force, a formal energy, "indigestible," a catalyst, a kind of colostomy, if by that we mean our insides are revealed, and nothing can ever, ever be concealed:

and me,
Threading my pursed-up way across the park,
An indigestible sterility.

Me. My. My form, my name, my threading together that sutures a world. Things fall apart, the roof caves in, but I have that: a name, a word to live by, work that I've designed.

Larkin's ending in "Spring" makes me think of Parker, in ways both expected and not. After dissonance and stasis, the beginning of a new poem, more energized, written by Surrey or Hopkins or even a bird, one who sees the excess, sees all, sees "Spring, of all seasons most gratuitous." Pop vision. Excess. Me in the midst of all. Selfie season; sorry, Surrey.

See the way that form can never fully confine

fold of untaught flower . . . race of water
earth's most multiple, excited daughter

This is Spring. A poet is in bloom like a tulip. But poets are guns, too. Call them modernists, indigestible sterilities, those who know they live amid ruined churches and bare ruin'd choirs. Fires. It's only those (like Larkin, like Bird) who know Spring, who know Life, who embrace their *me,* their *my.* The poem announces its end but it's only just beginning. The form has been breached. The cuppeth it runneth over and the cathedral collapseth. Parker blows his horn and there is a glory that is a kind of violence. This is poetry of excess—by the extraneous, the superfluous. Am I? I am. I am Warhol never turning off his camera. I am Parker never finishing his solo.

And those she has least use for see her best,
. . . . .
Their visions mountain-clear, their needs immodest.

Asked to explain what he liked so much about this ending, Larkin loses patience: "Isn't it clear? It means that these people, these indigestible sterilities, see rebirth and resurrection most vividly and imaginatively, but it isn't for them." The poet takes up the modern lament—sterility, old hat, that—but now remixed and transformed. It means new vision now for those who see it, like blind young Larkin with his peculiar pop vision. X-ray glasses ordered from some pulp magazine. *Peg's Paper*? Maybe.

A final word?

"I don't think that's a particularly good poem, though there are some nice things in it. I like the last few lines."

And endings are everything, maybe the only thing.

But that's no way to end.

Larkin, you built a room on the page, caged in by your sonnets. Did you know Charlie was on the road while you wrote? No. What could you know? So much less is known than unknown, isn't it?

His daughter is dying. It's 1954. A little older than Julia Warhola's baby girl: pneumonia. Charlie Parker is writing lines, like you, as you proof "Spring," your sonnet. Charlie Parker is writing lines like you. Fourteen, in fact. When you look at them laid out. Fourteen lines. Like a sonnet. Charlie is sending a telegram! His daughter is dying. His daughter is dead.

March 7, 1954. Charlie sends four telegrams from LA to New York. An Autobiography in a Telegram. To his wife, Chan, from 4:11 a.m. to 7:58 a.m. You can measure the time, you can mea-

sure the time. Fourteen lines. They add up. To what? A sonnet. A telegram. A death. A life. He'll die in exactly one year and five days from the writing of this. It all happens by accident. Call it Charlie Parker's "Aubade." By accident. Do we create and live and love and die by anything else?

Charlie is writing a telegram and near the couplet, near the end, near the end of his accidental sonnet, not teased out in "obscurity," two lines on flight and what is possible and what is not as we look about and see the night, and how I wish he sent it to you, Philip—how I wish he wrote you his accidental sonnet!—because I think you'd understand, after the bombs and the raids and the curfews and the night and the dog who makes off with the child's arm, I think you'd understand, Philip, (you must have understood) why art can look and feel so broken, so broken like a broken couplet, broken like a broken couple, broken like a bombed-out church, broken but still there, broken but still there's a form and it stands, still stands, still stands, and in the end you're not left with nothing, nothing, nothing, in the end you're not left with nothing because—look! it's there! look! look!—an image, a name, an elegy, a word:

MY DAUGHTER IS DEAD. I KNOW IT. I WILL BE THERE AS QUICK AS I CAN. MY NAME IS BIRD.

4
The Memory of Film

What Was Seen When We Saw

Is he blind?

What do we see when we say we see?

When we remember what we saw, what do we say?

A scratched wall? A book of life?

Is he, as some have said, a "figure of rapture," or is he in pain? Lost?

What is above him? What hangs just out of frame?

A broom—is it?—sweeps behind him, and we move with him left to right but, no, the legible dream is not that at all.

Does the machine—the camera, the photograph, the cinematic projector—allow for a rhapsody that we've somehow forgotten? Something that wants to linger, look up, not progress from left to right at all?

We move as we we've been taught but perhaps this hieroglyphic page is something else. Requiring from us, together, a new eye, a shared dream to dream this boy into being.

Perhaps he wants us to look up.

Isn't he waiting, waiting for a ball he's tossed, high, higher, high enough that now it's now suspended forever above the photo's frame?

I think of Warhol and his fits as a child. His mother's patience. Scissors, scissoring the movie stars from magazines, like his mother scissoring tin cans. Teaching him to read with scissors. America where anything was possible. Flowers.

I'm struck by the feeling of limitation here. Of blindness, yes, but the feeling, too, of feeling; the feeling of a hand on a wall, the way we orient ourselves and find direction, our eyes closed, awake to the dream.

We remember together, wounded. We look on those byzantine Byzantine icons of his mother the immigrant, the woman from the old country who reminds her son and maybe all of us that we are human and therefore connected and therefore capable of sharing our burdens and thus enduring them.

"Poetry makes nothing happen: it survives," says W. H. Auden at the death of Yeats. "And each in the cell of himself," Auden writes and looks about, "is almost convinced of his freedom." Still, the poet must "persuade us to rejoice."

We must be persuaded, reminded, each in our cells, because we are like that. Feeling unknown, we reach, a single hand, for a wall, a flower, a poem, and feel our way.

Since 1895 we've depended on film to guide us, even after it blinds us. We have faith in it, even after it shows us the planes going into the buildings, the bodies falling to the ground. For what else will save us?

We know there is another place, a better place, because there must be.

Or is that just a lyric from a song you forget you remember?

We remember seeing films as a child. We're sure we did. Now we're tired. Kids binge on *The Andy Griffith Show*, maybe. Andy and Aunt Bee. A to B. They learn to read. But once things were different. At least it seemed so.

We think we remember being held there, in a theater, a space of myth, next to our mother. We watched the screen.

That memory leads us on. We looked up.

We look up.

Manhattan Redeemed

Manhatta

Begin again. Begin here.

In the 1920s, just as in 2020, the city was thought to be over, done, doomed, machinery's flower, standardized, rigid—*or so said a group of cultural nationalists—scary word, that—who had rather fixed notions themselves about film, the city, and what the former might do to the latter. To renew it. Restore it.*

To bring it back to life.

This is their story, the story of film, poetry, and art. The story of artists wanting to do something. To begin again.

It's a story that needs telling, a bit long, perhaps . . . but it needs telling now in a moment when technology, art, and our sense of ourselves again interlock—or do they? Is art still part of the equation? Once it was. Perhaps that's what we're missing now. We know we want something, and maybe it's technology that can help, but we are wary, wary. What should we call it? Community? Nation? God, no. Citizenship? Belonging?

They were wary, too. The War had ended. The young century had bestowed the screen and they thought surely something great awaited. Some rough beast slouching? No, they didn't see that. Not yet. The century was still young. They had visions of Whitman—like Allen Ginsberg, in a supermarket, beneath the neon, later:

> I wandered in and out of the brilliant stacks of cans
> following you

The brilliants cans are following Walt. Cans of peaches. Cans of soup. The poet is, too. Andy's mother is on the water. A country is closing its border. It is 1921. She will call herself an American. These artists did, too. This was a long time ago. They were against the War that killed so many. Many were immigrants. This was a long time ago. Others told them where it was all going. Dadaists. Surrealists. Others told them where it was all going.

But they wanted a say. They thought of themselves as Americans. They wanted to say. Say what?

Where are we going, Walt Whitman?

We forget these artists.

But we shouldn't.

Part 1: Who Made Pop?

See the masked man.
  It's a holdup.
  See the Dadaists and the Surrealists.
  It's a holdup.

At least, that's what they saw, and that's what they did, those Europeans who first invented American popular culture, as the poet Louis Aragon liked to claim. They who dragged themselves from the War, from its wounds, from the old into the new; they who were killed by flu (Apollinaire), gassed (Léger), and had arms removed (Cendrars): still, they came. To tell the land of the machine about the machine.

The machine was the heart of America, and Americans didn't know it, couldn't understand it, insecure country that it was, blundering into the world, into the century. Or, at least that's what the Dadaists and the Surrealists came to say. And the most American of machines was the cinema—an upstart technology, a Western outlaw, to which the arts of the Old World were only too happy, too happy to surrender.

Or, at least that's how Aragon's fellow Surrealist Philippe Soupault dramatized it in his essay from 1923, "The U.S.A. Cinema":

> *At every street corner [a poster of] a man, his face covered with a red handkerchief, leveled a revolver at the peaceful passerby. We imagined . . . the roar of motors, explosions, and cries of death. We rushed into the cinemas, and realized immediately that everything had changed.*

But there's something left out of this account, an account by now well known—of how film taught the arts, as one critic puts it, "speed, simultaneity . . . and visceral shock." Left out are those artists who wanted it all to slow down, who wanted—and they didn't have another name for it—*art.*

The country had so much, too much, but so little art. And they thought of themselves as Americans.

The offspring of these American artists would not look like them. It's hard to trace a family resemblance, but they are family nonetheless. Their offspring would make a five-hour film of a sleeping man (and call it *Sleep*); they would film skyscrapers through the night, which people would call epic (half-serious, half-joking).

Their offspring would not look like them. These artists were tinkerers, amateurs, really. And they are left out of accounts of modern art and literature and film that were first shaped by Dadaists, Surrealists; first shaped by the wounded men, men dreaming of bombs.

Their offspring would not look like them. But, then again, perhaps pop culture is not what it seems, is not a fever dream at all, or not just that. Perhaps it's not just a holdup, a stickup, a death race. Perhaps it dreams, at times, like Hart Crane, like Andy Warhol, of bridges and buildings. "I think of cinemas," writes Crane at the start of *The Bridge,* his epic invocation. He would make the attempt. Do what film could have done if it had not lost its way.

Their offspring would not look like them, perhaps, but then again maybe they do if we only look again. Slow down. Look. We could do worse than to know them and to learn that pop—and us, and Andy, and so much else—also came from this. From Whitman. From them.

The little magazine the *Seven Arts* (1916–1917) embodied what Ann Douglas calls "the prewar Zeitgeist of troubled Whitmanesque prophecy and idealism." Troubled, because faith in the power of art to redeem and to heal was strained by this simple thought: Industrialized America was speeding past the point of redemption. Fast.

These concerns brought together critics. Randolph Bourne, Kenneth Macgowan, Van Wyck Brooks, and the journal's founding editors (Waldo Frank and James Oppenheim) considered themselves heirs to William Morris and to Whitman. The *Seven Arts* circle thought technology was a potentially expressive force, but it lacked one thing: guidance from artists.

Call it a measured embrace, what these Americans wanted. Whatever it was, it blurred the line between art and machines, evident in the journal's first essay on film. There the cinema is an "an art that won't behave."

The phrase conjures authoritarian fantasies. How to make it behave? Why make it behave at all? But perhaps behave is the wrong word. They wanted film to breathe, like Andy shooting, shooting, shooting all night long. Like watching John Giorno sleep in *Sleep*. Could film do that? They wondered, in their own way, in the years before Andy was born. And they made a film that does just that, in 1921. They were cutting, cutting, while Julia was on the water, arriving in June. They called it *Manhatta.*

Can the artist's hand help us recover, remember the something we once forgot? It's complex, this regard for pop, we must admit. But maybe we must admit this, too: So is pop.

Call it a lost chapter in pop's history. Call it the interdisciplinary past, if you must. Whatever it is, there's something about film and art we've chosen to neglect. Now, one hundred years on, in this moment of AI, when borders close again, and new media forms promise to transform (or erase?) the arts, when Martin Scorsese complains that films are no longer art but "perfect products manufactured for immediate consumption," we could do worse than remember this legacy. It's a legacy of critique and creative collaboration.

Many were immigrants, many against the War, the closing of borders. Many were associated with *The Masses,* the journal on the side of labor, strikers. But they called themselves Americans. And they wanted to make the cinema—or maybe the machine, or maybe urban-industrial modernity—behave.

Must we call them naïve?

Why Behave? *American Studies: A Primer* *Why Be Good?*

Film, they thought, was more than a disorienting technology for the arts to imitate or ignore. Film, they thought, depended upon the arts as tutor-texts, upon artists as tutors. They believed they could be film's teachers, and teach the machine how to rein in, revive, reinvigorate not the political body but communal life. What Whitman meant by the word *En-Masse.*

It takes some work, but you can trace the contours of this attempt in the poetry of the *Seven Arts,* in the works of artists close to the journal—John Sloan's painting *Movies, Five Cents* (1907), for example, one of the country's first about film. And you can see it best in Paul Strand and Charles Sheeler's *Manhatta* (1921), a short film that for a long time was forgotten. It is a film about a dream of unity, a holistic (call it epic) vision of the New York cityscape. *En-Masse.*

Manhatta is a film that gets transformed by Whitman's poetry; or maybe it makes more sense to say that it transforms, cuts, scissors together a new kind of Whitman, rewriting the urban and the industrial, like a poet, or like a poetic machine.

Not everyone thinks so, of course. It is slow, and fast times need fast books, or that's the way the thinking goes when it comes to film and art and modern life. But fast books read slow, slow us down, don't they? They make us look around, and up, up, and that's what *Manhatta* does, too.

A film can be a masked man, true; a holdup, a shakedown, as Soupault put it. That's what the critic Dickran Tashjian meant way back when by the "European reassessment" of US culture. That Eurovision has been central to our notions of art and pop ever since, and what one has to do with the other. But it's not the only account.

Once, there were artists who sought to transform the cinema into something else, a US, an indigenous art (a term chosen with Whitmanic purpose), free from European influence. Rather than surrender, rather than put their hands up, the poets, painters, and filmmakers in the milieu of the *Seven Arts* sought to influence film by critiquing its industrial art, its speed. They wanted to find its heart.

Does the screen need unacknowledged legislators, to impart a sense of restraint, rhythm, and order to render this world (hurrying into war and death and bombs and explosions) into something else? To render it legible? That's what they thought. To do as Whitman had done before them.

Scissors, like Julia Warhola's, make things new. These artist used scissors, too. To cut, to edit films. And to cut up Whitman's words and make him new. A poet after their image and likeness. A poet to bring to the machine a new understanding, a sense of restraint. That is what we do with art, after all. It becomes our equipment for living, a thing we use and do things to.

You must know some of this already, or feel it, or live in its remains. It's the complaint about low and high culture. The feeling that Marvel films aren't movies (because movies are art); the feeling that what passes for art in the excesses of this late-late-capitalist show, well, that leaves you wondering, too. As art critic Jerry Saltz puts it, writing in the shadow of the *Seven Arts*, "How does the art world live with itself?"

They wondered that, too. And they directed their sights on film, dreaming of a middle path, so simple, so childish-sounding precisely because it seems today so hard to believe—after the blood and the bombs ("it's the same old theme / since 19– . . .") and the Bauhaus and the art house and the international modernisms that bestow upon us the feeling that we're living in a prison. Well, to turn back now seems childish, suspicious. But this was before all of that. Their dream of a middle path was before all of that. They called it the Whitmanic middle, a more inclusive space made from both high and low.

Like the pop song says. *Meet me in the middle.* That's what they said Walt said, too. But what did it really mean?

According to James Oppenheim's first editorial in the *Seven Arts*, high and low, studio and street, muse and machine all stood to gain from this rapprochement. Reconciling "the art of subtlety" (high/art) with "the art of vitality" (low/movies) would "unify a nation and express a national identity."

Perhaps he was wrong. Naïve. But perhaps it was never tried, this dream of pop.

Why not?

Because it's hard, isn't it?

First, if there was ambivalence about bringing film into the economy of the traditional arts, it was because a real problem emerged. Film granted vitality, yes, the feeling of a more powerfully felt world, yes, but through a calculus of distraction, dislocation, and speed. The problem was speed, pure and simple: what Waldo Frank considered the "shrieking rhythm" of the puritan, the pioneer, and the industrialist, the unholy trinity of his *Our America* (1919) that made the land rich and the soul poor.

What to do about speed? How to make the cinema behave? If it didn't, there could be no middle tradition, no keeping of Whitman's promise that we escape the yoke of the machine.

They were vexed, in other words, and with good reason. But they were also intrigued, these early pop artists, and they were tempted to embrace the unruly machine, tempted to set a hand to it, to explore it, and to explore the street with it. Navigate the street, set its incoherence right.

But was it incoherent, the street? And what's that even mean? Did it need to be transcended? And how does one even go about doing that? These are questions we keep asking ourselves, it turns out. We keep asking our mother, our machines.

Your Mother Is a Machine: Transcendental Pop

Maybe Warhol can teach us. We see him picturing a building, the Empire State Building, say, and time is the only thing moving. Maybe that's what they meant, the *Seven Arts* artists. Maybe that's what they dreamt, these early Americans, dreaming of Whitman.

The machine was their mother, an image that turns up in their poems, in their paintings. I think of Julia Warhola. What do we want from her? We want to dream. We say to her: Tell us a bedtime story. And again I think of Terrence Malick, and children speaking to their mother before they sleep.

Tell us a story from before we can remember.

Isn't that what pop asks? What pop does? Gives you the soup can that is not a soup can at all. It is your mother.

What else does the mom in pop mean?

Here's a story, Mother says:

I went for a ride in a plane once.

I think of *The Tree of Life.* Flying machines. Transcendent machines. Storytelling machines. Your mother is a machine. Teach us to dream. And in your dream she flies like this.

Mother who flies. Mother who floats. And the children dream on as a voice-over intones:

Mother. Make me good. Make me brave.

Make me behave? Is that what the *Seven Arts* wanted?

Can we call it transcendental pop?

And isn't Warhol, too, at times, like this? Maybe all the time?

These are pop's spiritual practitioners, Warhol and Malick, dreamers, and surely they're not the only ones. Two artists who seem like they could not possibly be branches on the same family tree. Well, Julia Warhola's pantry is large. It contains multitudes.

Transcendence. Transcendence in and through the machine. This sounds, of course, embarrassing. Let's break the mood. Here's Michael Robbins on the age of drones:

This is for the drone-in-chief
. . . .
The bomb bay opens with a queef.

To speak of transcendence at a time like this. In an age of drones and GIFs, in what Steven Shaviro calls the age of post-cinematic affect. Sheesh.

A nation rolls its lonely eyes and tweets.

But thinking of cinemas, Hart Crane saw those lonely eyes, too.

With multitudes bent toward some flashing scene
Never disclosed, but hastened to again,
Foretold to other eyes on the same screen

He, too, shared the dream, called himself American, believed in a different destiny for the machine.

We can't turn our back. They ask us, still, to make sense of what they thought, and what they thought they were doing, and, finally, what they did.

What were they doing?

The art historian Wanda Corn:

> *Their dilemma was how to be modern and antimodern simultaneously or, to formulate it another way, how to be cultural leaders of machine age America without succumbing to its perceived evils.*

Did Andy ever feel that dilemma? Probably not.

And yet, the cinema appeared to them (as it surely did to him) to hover, almost float, like Malick's mother, magically, somewhere between machinery and art, between the traffic of the street and the silent harmony of nature, between fragmentation and a new-kind-of-never-before-thought-of-Whitman-sounding-sort-of unity.

They perished, of course. This could not last.

We can talk of their spark between 1907–1921 and that is generous, but the world of the *Seven Arts* crashed in the 1920s revolt against high culture, nationalist concerns (nation! imagine!) and any trace of mystical or aesthetic sloppiness. It's the same old story. They were swept away by upstarts, American Dadaists parodying the French, of course. Transatlantic *Broom* (1921–1924) had it in for them. Matthew Josephson, Harold Loeb and others proposed their own brash art of "the skyscrapers, of the movies, of the streets" as a corrective to the "Russian-realism, American soil spirit" of the *Seven Arts*. What was that "American soil spirit"? Folk? Like tin cans turned into flowers?

It doesn't sound so bad, does it?

Well, we'll never know, because caricature wins the day, and we're the poorer for it.

Our sense of film's place in the artistic practice of an earlier age is impoverished. As a result, our cinema is, too. Yes, the cinema was always anarchy, but it was also shelter from the storm. The film historian Tom Gunning reminds us of this. In the beginning, both revolution and respite in early film. Film gave "the stimuli of a new modern life—finding within it, alternately, balance and harmony or chaos and apocalypse." In this careful marriage, pop was born; beneath these twin stars, pop came of age, guided in part by dreamers tracing a frenetic screen—tracing unceasing motion, crowds, parts, and pieces. They trusted, like Whitman, it was part of a grander design.

Their dream reached its peak in 1921 with *Manhatta*, the nation's first avant-garde film. But that term is wrong. It was art for people, plain and simple, strange but beautiful. In a country closing its border. But that dream ended.

Who knows when it began? Let's turn to an avid moviegoer in 1908. (He's painting the movies.)

Part 2. Painting the Movies

Here's a diary entry from John Sloan, the painter of urban life crowned "the historian of New York" on the pages of the *Seven Arts*.

> February 22, 1908:
> *Walked up Broadway. A beautiful day. Washington's Birthday—and everyone seemed to be out. Watched a moving picture photographer set up his camera. He waited and I did also to see what he was after. Soon around 34th Street, into Broadway, turned a little parade—Volunteer Firemen of the old days of New York.*

You can almost see the Ken Burns close-up, can't you? Hear the talking head take to the screen. To say that, well, Sloan's entry isn't all that surprising. Sloan's canvases had been attempting to capture film's immediacy for a while. This shouldn't surprise us (although it does).

We who are raised under the sign of the modern, under the sign of Duchamp's 1913 Armory explosion, sense that surely nothing, nothing came before that. But we also know, surely, that history is wrong. Much is erased; much is forgotten.

Much is erased; much is forgotten. An immigrant, a woman, Theresa Bernstein started with Sloan the Society for Independent Artists, and was part of the Philadelphia Ten. Do you know her? Do you know them? They were painters from the School of Design for Women my sister attended in Philadelphia, the college where I modeled for drawing classes as a child, where I stood on Saturdays holding my arrow and bow.

Much is erased; much is forgotten. Weren't painters like Bernstein and Sloan attempting, simply, to capture the street? Can't we call them our early pop artists, tracing the surfaces to see what it all might mean? Some, like Sloan, brought the cinema to the canvas; most did not. But the screen simply set the scene for what was to become American art. Everyone was setting up. Playing their part. Awaiting the parade, believing in pop. That should not surprise us (although it does).

Earlier that month in 1908, Sloan exhibited what appears to be the first American painting to address the cinema and its promise for the nation: *Movies, Five Cents.* Along with work by members of "The Eight," Sloan's painting hung on the walls of New York City's Macbeth Galleries, February 3, 1908, the inaugural exhibition of what became the Ashcan School. Ashcan as in trashcan, as in the pot you piss in and the window you throw it out of. Of course, it was an insult, and it was an honor; they were deemed anti-genteel, painters after Whitman, many of them Philadelphia journalists, sketching the everyday, inspired by Robert Henri who challenged them to get real. Real "as the clods of horse-shit and snow" mucking their boots, he'd say. Surface matters. That's where you find the horse-shit and the snow. Their brushstrokes: athletic. To show the show, the real show. The horse-shit and the snow. No need to go to Europe for that.

But the quick account of a painter watching the filming of a parade—an "actuality," the most popular genre of film's first decade—remains a startling voice from the archive, doesn't it? You can't unhear it. At the start of a century in search of a national, unifying art, there was a relationship, it's clear, between high and low, art and film.

If we think of early cinema, it's not about artists like Sloan or parades; for too long we've thought of those primitive moviegoers before us, scared and startled by oncoming trains. But that's changed. We now see them as free, as giving themselves over to the screen where anything and everything could happen—a cinema of abandonment to an unfolding world. As Mary Ann Doane puts it in *The Emergence of Cinematic Time*: "Contingency itself was a display."

It's odd, isn't it?, the cinema's realization of modernity's Enlightenment dream. Total representation. The inscription of time itself, no details lost, none subordinate to any other. Surrealists and Dadaists could not get enough of this. And they were not wrong. But it was really the Italian Futurists who were most enchanted, the Futurists who dreamt, also, by the way, of slaughtering the past. The cinema could be used to do just that. What would Sloan say?

Let's leave him waiting there, waiting for the parade.

Pop: Futurist Dance or the Flintstone Flop?

F. T. Marinetti's "The Technical Manifesto of Futurist Literature" (1912) is obsessed with film. Why? As a model for new poetic practice. Abolish "the ridiculous inanity of the old syntax inherited from Homer." Flat-footed prosody gets outpaced by the rush of modern life: "Just enough to walk, take a short run, and come up short, panting!" This is speed-mania to burst the confines of syntax. Burst the limits of mind. The limits of body, too. In other words, film says, this is a stickup, the past is dead. Long live the Future. Do the Futurists see that there will be blood? It's hard to say. They imagine a dance.

> *Film offers us the dance of an object that disintegrates and recomposes itself without human intervention. It offers the backward sweep of a diver whose feet fly out of the sea and bounce violently back on the springboard. Finally, it offers the sight of a man driving at 200 kilometers per hour. All these represent the movements of matter which are beyond the laws of human intelligence, and hence of an essence which is more significant.*

And this was early cinema, too. Buildings rising from their own ashes only to be destroyed again. One thinks of films like *Demolishing and Building Up the Star Theatre* (1901), time-lapse photography and the exhibitor's flair for running films backwards. This was the Future. Creative-destruction (heavy on the latter).

Compared to this, Sloan's account is even odder. There's incredible reserve ("He waited and I did also") and a formal volta, the way the street "turned a little parade." No mechanical sleight of hand; the order is *in* the cityscape, revealed if you watch and if you wait with the steady eye of the camera. Hardly pop? Too old-fashioned, right? But not if we call it old school, if we think about the artist on the street.

Doesn't pop do precisely this? And maybe only this? Wait and intervene in moments of our forgetting? Isn't that what we mean by *old school* after all? Yes, pop's a Futurist dance. But you also walk like an Egyptian, like all sorts of things that are human. Pop remembers, recalls, throws back, archives, makes mixes, remixes, and course corrects, of course, like a painter waiting, like a machine waiting, like a Beastie Boy rapping on "Intergalactic": "I am known to do the Wop" (and also, a line later, "the Flintstone Flop"). The Flop is based on an old cartoon, a kind of Futurist dance, true, but out of our past, our pop. It's not that the Futurists were wrong about breaking dance, breaking poems, breaking art. It's that pop remembers, recounts, recalls the human touch; pop aligns itself with memory and the orders of memory.

It's there, in other words, if you just look. Continuity between past and present, streets haunted by ghosts even ("Volunteer Firemen of the old days of New York") as painter and filmmaker look upon, their looking a kind of pop homage. This will be, more or less, the vision of Strand and Sheeler in *Manhatta*. People call it a documentary, but it's how they build a new kind of bridge between then and now, ghosts, ghost of

Whitman, of hands that build and built New York, Mohawks walking iron, the Lenape, so many, so many. The film takes scissors to the "n" and returns the island, too. Returns it to roots, to the pop imaginary of the past.

Whose *Manhatta*? The question of audience matters. No painter matched Sloan's gift for capturing the city at the intersection between machines and the audiences they construct, the audiences that they imagine (and the audience that we imagine ourselves to be a part of: Whitman's *En-Masse*). This intersection is intimate in *Movies, Five Cents*. Find the image online and find your seat before the screen.

The gallery-going experience here is linked to the moviegoing experience. What did people think, seeing this crowded room of moviegoers—spectators, new gallery-goers—hanging in a gallery? There's a play of mirrors here.

Linking gallery and movies was pretty common, actually. America's earliest film theory—the kind that appeared in the *Seven Arts*—looked to the museum. How to make an action scene? Vachel Lindsay in *The Art of the Moving Picture* (1915): "Go to any museum. Find the Parthenon room."

This was, after all, the age of the tableau, and the thought that cinema might set into motion the sculptural (and vice versa) is right there in the thick frame around Sloan's film screen. The cinema did its work by framing a moving world. Spectators could read it in a way that its participants could not.

And yet, Sloan's painting is about the promise of participation. Call it Whitmanic. Welcome to the body politic. See the arresting gaze of the woman at the painting's center command your attention. This place, yes, can lead to distraction (or slumber—note the man sleeping to her left). But there's something about a gaze at the dead (living) center of the picture.

There's an invitation here. Exit signs are clearly marked. But why leave?

You are asked to join: the crowd, the screen—all narratives promising unity. If you know Sloan, you know this is one of his tropes, his tricks: regulate distraction through the attentive face in the crowd. It's a neat trick, to bring order, meaning, and even personal communion to an otherwise illegible cityscape. I'm speaking to you, says Sloan. Like Whitman, who waits for you, reader. Where? Beneath the sole of your shoe. Look. In the clods of horse-shit and snow. A neat trick, but perhaps there's something more to it.

Look up. In Sloan's imagining, film underwrites order, or rather overwrites it; look up, the screen literally models intimate contact. This is important. What can feel like an unbridgeable overhead divide between machine and human is another Sloan trope. El trains rocket by on the bridge over your head in some paintings. But here that gets gently, softly undone. No divide between us and the machine, after all. The screen's whites, blues, and yellows get softened, softened in the hatband of the gazing woman, in the blouse of the smiling young woman in the lower right-hand corner of the painting.

That she's African American, the smiling young woman, matters. Pop happens in a communal space for Sloan. He was illustrator for *The Masses.* His searing covers skewered the hypocrisy of his country. Here are millionaires at the opera (he called them "the unemployed") and, there, in his most famous cover, is the Ludlow Massacre, where children were murdered by the National Guard at a coal mining strike in Colorado.

That she's African American matters. This, for Sloan, was an inclusive space, or could be. A site for screening and archiving race, showing the drama, struggle, and victories. Sloan's diary, again, on the prizefighting film *Johnson-Ketchel Fight* (1909)—one of many made of the famous heavyweight champion Jack Johnson:

> *The big black spider gobbled up the small white fly—aggressive fly—wonderful to have this event repeated. Some day the government will wake up to the necessity of establishing a library of Biograph films as history.*

The voice of the archive; the faith that what pop does is archive; that one day we may very well remember the old school. Let it teach us. Pop remembers. The screen is a link to the past—to link future generations to Johnson's conquest "as history"—because we must not forget. Forget what? Us. That this is us. The smiling woman in the back row is also dreaming of you dreaming of the screen that is dreaming, in turn, of her.

Painters like Sloan mirrored this dream on canvas. It was Whitman's dream, Henri's dream seen in his portrait of a paperboy, Willie Gee, whose mother was born into slavery. Look at *Portrait of Willie Gee* (1904), the child holding an apple; place it next to Alfred Stieglitz's photo (two decades later) of Waldo Frank, the critic carving his apples, too. This is not Henri's *Laughing Child* (1907), the face a riot of brushstrokes and force. There is, instead, restraint here, dignity even (especially) in the newsboy, the feeling of Henri's professional respect for his work, day in and day out, delivering the news to the painter like the painters were doing (in their own way), many of them brought up in the trade. And see Frank's shoes turn in, almost childish, his hat pressed down, his lips turned up in what is almost a smile? Waldo and Willie meet across two decades here, linked by the *Seven Arts*. These are scraps from our history. Just scraps. Like the apples in both paintings. But those, of course, are the most important parts. We are what we eat. What we consume is what we share: an apple, a can of soup. This is communion. This, too, is pop.

Part 3. Beyond the Screen

And what about the poets?

Whitman's disciples, wanting to describe the strangeness of the world around them; for them, too, the cinema was an invitation to the machine age, a door through which to enter the modern. And when they arrived outside? They imagined the street was a screen. And the street (and the screen) could and should be beautiful.

Exit through the Gift Shop

Poetry about film can be an act of resistance, a form of criticism that takes the shape of Martin Scorsese's criticism of Marvel films, actually. When Scorsese writes that Marvel films "lack something essential to cinema: the unifying vision of an individual artist. Because, of course, the individual artist is the riskiest factor of all," he dials in the legacy of the *Seven Arts*, its critical engagement with market forces and the role of the artist. Who will be Virgil in the pop inferno? We need a guide because film is always losing its way. In 1907. In 2020. Its forms and thrills as increasingly mechanical as the age it embodied, said the *Seven Arts*. And that's what Scorsese says, too: "If people are given only one kind of thing and endlessly sold only one kind of thing, of course they're going to want more of that one kind of thing." Scorsese raised eyebrows, but what he expressed is rooted in the Whitmanic middle tradition, its faith in art, its wariness of the machine.

The screen didn't simply need to repeat and reproduce the impoverished experience of the modern for audiences who were already exploited by industry. This is where artists came in, closing their eyes, heading for the exits, and reimagining the screen as a space of beauty, yes, but abstraction, too, and to use Scorsese's word: "risk."

Here's a teenager writing during the First World War:

The last pose flickered, failed. The screen's dead white
Glared in a sudden flooding of harsh light
Stabbing the eyes; and as I stumbled out
The curtain rose.

Stephen Vincent Benét's "Rain After a Vaudeville Show" reads like the journal's manifesto on pop, beginning where the show ends. Alliteration ruptures, caesuras, too, and we're made to feel the assault. There's a hitch in the step even of the poet who trips, can't quite get a grip. Here pop is false mother, something that smothers. In fact, "the choking smother" sends the poet running for air, but he won't leave the cinema, not yet. The lobby is shelter, cover, a place to see a different kind of motion, like Ralph Steiner filming water, like Warhol filming sleep. The screen is out there as well, poets discovered. It's called the street.

I stepped into the lobby—and stood still
Struck dumb by sudden beauty, body and will.
Cleanness and rapture—excellence made plain—
The storming, thrashing arrows of the rain!

This is a poem, like so many are, of wet surfaces, and new screens, and better screens. But it's also about motion and looking closely at things. The rain provides participles: motion, a fluid moving, a corrective to the stumbling, a natural rhythmic counterpoint. The "sudden flooding" of piercing "arrows" are no longer a "stabbing" vision but cut to the quick, make "plain" new vision. The outside is critical counter-screen.

This is a poem of *photogénie*, what French film critics were beginning to theorize around this same time: beauty produced by film's flow, a sublime instant, a new way of seeing. John Giorno, in Warhol's *Sleep*, slowly turns. Look! The shock of sudden beauty functions like a refrain in Benét's poem. This, too, is pop, these transformations, this grappling and patience. You wait for it. Beauty: "Beauty strove suddenly, and rose, and flowered."

Art historians have taught us something about the weather. Rain, sleet, fog, and snow were tools to do something new to the urban landscape. It reminds me of that *Onion* article that makes the rounds at the first sign of snowflakes:

Blanket of Snow Creates Illusion That Town Not a Total Shithole

True. But it's worth remembering Henri's "clods of horse-shit and snow," the smell of streets one hundred years ago, and the way that poets started to glide about the surface of things, doodling, making quick jots, like William Carlos Williams and his doctor's notes, like Pound in a subway station, like poets on wet streets trafficking in new illusions, like a puddle you look down upon, tying your shoe, and there it is, the sky, look!, looking back at you.

This was Whitman's dream, reflected back in startling images. By 1917, the last year of Amy Lowell's Imagist anthologies, the Imagist movement had been watered down. Sure, join an undergrad workshop today and see the puddles of that wet dream. But was it once something else? Whitman at heart? A dream of unity (Pound's "petals on a wet, black bough"—petals, yes, but one bough) for those who worked hard to see? While Benét's couplets are a far cry from early Imagism, "Rain After a Vaudeville Show" riffs on the movement's more common tropes, if not John Gould Fletcher's most famous lines:

Flickering of incessant rain
On flashing pavements:

Sudden scurry of umbrellas:
Bending, recurved blossoms of the storm.

Imagism is about restraint: show don't tell, we're told (and told again). But it's also about poems curving in new ways, bending to connect to the energy of the pop culture "flickering" and "flashing" about. The screen is the street, the street is the screen. There, for those who look, is a new energy, beauty, and even depth. Surfaces pop.

Still, your town very well may be a shithole. It's true. And Pictorialism, that gospel of beauty practiced for a while by Stieglitz, was a kind of prettifying after all, an erasure with snow, a blurring, an Insta-filter to ignore dimmer, darker realities. Sure. Everyone loves your selfies, but you know better, don't you? To talk of transcendence at a time like this! People said that, and still do. They said it about Stieglitz, and American painters, and poets, and still do. Look at all they ignored. To write poems at a time like this. They still do.

And yet, what does it mean to reflect, to see a door where there was no door before, a mirror in a surface, a sky in a puddle, a reflection in a fender? Is that only an escape by an escape artist? Or can it be a new reckoning with the surfaces of things, things that connect us to everything, to each other? This is a working definition of pop and art.

Once, I saw a beautiful film at the Hammer Museum in Los Angeles, *Visions of a City* (1957): Larry Jordan shoots the glassy, mirrored surfaces of San Francisco's shop windows and car fenders to reflect both the city and the poet Michael McClure. Things blur and become one.

And then there's May Swenson in the *New Yorker*, New Year's Eve issue, the end of 1960, a riotous shape-shifting decade ahead. What do such poems mean? This film dream? These surfaces? Swenson's "At the Museum of Modern Art" teaches you how to look. Sit in the lobby. Watch the street:

And there's a mesmeric experimental film

constantly reflected on the flat side of the wide
steel-plate pillar opposite the crenellated window.

A film about what? You forget to ask by the time you get your mind around the plosive bulk of modern life (plate/pillar/opposite). A film about what? Don't ask what is it. It's a new mirror of the everyday. That's all that it is: its ugliness, shallowness, but not just that. The surfaces of pop make us peculiarly aware of surfaces as such, which means the things we ignore. Things that are constantly there, against which we think we must fortify ourselves lest we . . . despair? Will we? Do we? What happens when we look? We don't escape, we no longer want to. We find new rhythms. New ways to be in this world.

Experimental cinema may not have been on Babette Deutsch's mind, writing so many years before in the *Seven Arts*. But the 1960s can be found there, too: Swenson and her lobby view. This is pop. This is lineage. Swenson was but a child in 1916. Born into war. Meanwhile, Deutsch, born with the cinema in 1895, knows to look for something more: the surfaces beneath her feet, the reflections on the street. What business does she have writing her "Magic Screen" at a time like this?

Deutsch's "Magic Screen" is another meditation on the modern cityscape; it's about art's imaginative access, what it cuts up in new abstractions. Her screen is a rain-slicked street where you can see a kaleidoscopic natural order beneath the rush of foot, hoof, and wheel. This is abstraction before New Yorkers knew to call it that; before Iris Barry at the MoMA screened mesmeric films in galleries, divorcing the screen from the world of pop, the world from which it came. Maybe we should remember to put them back there, like Swenson does, as we stand in museums, lost in our heads (and phones). Put the films and the poems back on the street, on the steel-plate pillars, in the clods of horse-shit and snow. You are horse-shit, you poems and films, and to horse-shit back you shall go. That's Whitman's prayer. Here's Deutsch, and there's the horses, and see them go like Muybridge's dream:

Under the wheels and hooves and hurrying feet
The darkly-shining pave
Reaches into the night.
On blackness color flames: purple and blurs of red.

A poem about living in the blur. Here the blur of the city is a smudge, a blot, "as though crushed / emeralds bled," not free from pain, violence, but also bleeding into a new kind of transcendence. There is magic in Deutsch's ode and in all of these poems that cinema will do well to remember, then and now. Writing about how film embraces or, better, chases the urban experience. There's risk, as Scorsese puts it. Unknowing, too.

Art like this is inspired by cinema, we can be sure, but it attempts to inspire it, too (and we forget this, this boldness on the artist's part). Is that still with us? Of course, in every amateur attempt, every earnest mistake. These artists made those mistakes first. Who were they, looking down at their feet, unlacing their shoes like Dr. Williams, doodling notes? They who wove formal fragments—clipped lines, blurs of light and motion—into a larger, more powerful unity, like Deutsch does here: they gave us Swenson and the experimental tradition, and a brand of pop that maybe we forget to claim as our own.

But it is. And we should.

Part 4. Epic So Epic

At once an urban documentary and an Imagist photoplay, Paul Strand and Charles Sheeler's *Manhatta* is a short comprised of sixty-five shots of the city's harbor, buildings, transport, and people. It took a bit to become *Manhatta,* to find a name that fit. It premiered as the "scenic" component of a larger vaudeville and film program at New York's Rialto Theater on July 24, 1921, under the (slightly more empirical) title *New York, the Magnificent.* That was probably given by the theater itself.

1921. Summer. Julia Warhola arrives in June. It's the year the nation shuts down immigration. Nation on guard. Nation on watch. Watchmen. In Tulsa, that summer, the burning of Black Wall Street: destruction, terror, and mayhem. One hundred years on and we remember, pop remembers. We watch *Watchmen* in 2019 and remember. What we didn't know? Or what we wanted to forget? A summer of burning cities. White terror. Wall Street bombed the year before. Markets tumbled. Wall Street walls crumbled. Was this a time for artists to reimagine their cities? At a time like this? That's what the artists around the *Seven Arts* thought.

Where Are We Going, Walt?

The film's name changed again when it was screened at a 1923 Dada soirée in Paris as *Fumée de New York,* and finally became *Manhatta* in its 1927 appearance at the London Film Society. In a way, the title regressed from bricks and mortar of New York through misty smoke and into the remote past (or was it the future?) of Manhatta (or Mannahatta). And this is symbolic: The film itself almost disappeared into formalist ether.

But scholars, essayists, film historians, and artists have brought it back.

Film histories gave *Manhatta* "short shrift," Jan-Christopher Horak notes: "a series of static photographs." No more. But we still don't know what to make of Whitman's poetry in the film. And that's for a simple reason. If we don't know the past, and the legacy of the *Seven Arts*, we don't know what these artists wanted from their pop culture. But we do know. And the poetry makes sense.

1. The poetry rewrites the film's scattered city into the most ancient and nationalistic of verse forms, the epic. It's signaled by the twelve-part poetic structure of *Manhatta*. This isn't "a simple, poetic documentary," as one critic put it; we're sailors here, arriving, immigrants, even. We're navigating the shoals, we're charting the founding of a city-state. Something new.
2. This is a film about making, about labor, about *poiesis*: The labor of the city (we watch cranes lifting, spinning like giant movie cameras) is metaphor, sure, but it also doubles the work of the poetic narrative. Both function as sites of construction and digs that uncover in the present the past. And the past is what heals.
3. "Mannahatta," hailed in Whitman's poem by that same name (as the city's "aboriginal name"), functions for the poet as a magic signifier; it materializes its referent, its doubled consonants "nesting" the word like the water around the city. "I see that word nested in nests of water-bays, superb," writes Whitman about the city, about the word. This is verbal vision, a conjuring.

4. Whitman's "Mannahatta" is about the blur of word/world. It appealed to Strand who claimed for his camera a transcendent capacity to claim "absolute unqualified objectivity." This is verbal vision, a conjuring of the real.

Consisting of long-shots and close-ups, *Manhatta* is bifocal; it's a new way of seeing; it's a transcendental vision that tries to complete the popular project of the *Seven Arts*.

In this sense, it is the dream of poets, photographers, and painters reading Whitman with scissors, like Warhol after them. They crop, repurpose, redeem what's left to redeem in a nation that, in the summer of 1921, is bleeding.

Bleeding.

Directors Cut: Reading Whitman with Scissors

How to make Whitman a prophet of the movie camera, the detached, patient, spiritual machine?

Meet the new Whitman. He prefers his solitude to joining the crowd, witnessing the splendor of the modern city more than participating in it. The film's second intertitle—and first use of the poem, "A Broadway Pageant"—makes just this point: "When million-footed Manhattan / unpent, descends / to its pavements" introduces the commuting/crowd sequence, a quote that carefully scissors out the poet's response to this vision ("I too arising, answering, descend to the pavements, merge with the crowd, and gaze with them"). Not pop, perhaps, or at least how we've come to think of it. But then again it does remind us of Warhol's distance from things ("I don't want to get too close; I don't like to touch things"), his lack of touch, which allowed things to be seen as they truly were.

This is not the Whitman of the street; rather, like Andy watching, watching, this is the Whitman of "Sparkles from the Wheel," a Whitman of quiet restraint, of Strand-like photographic focus. Recall "Sparkles," that other Whitman, the poet of control, which finds its equivalent in a knife-grinder. The grinder's careful mastery of his machine produces "Sparkles from the wheel."

Withdrawn I join a group of children watching, I pause
aside with them.
By the curb toward the edge of the flagging,
A knife-grinder works at his wheel sharpening a great
knife,
. . . .
The scene and all its belongings, how they seize and
affect me,
The sad sharp-chinn'd old man with worn clothes and
broad shoulder-band of leather,
Myself effusing and fluid, a phantom curiously floating,
now here absorb'd and arrested,
The group, (an unminded point set in a vast
surrounding,)

Cut. Cut nice, said Julia about Andy, her son. Did Whitman teach Strand and Sheeler how to cut, how to edit? Did they find new license for their own oblique angles in this "floating" perspective? Perhaps we forget this Whitman, this widescreen view—elevated, detached, mobile—that lets the "group" get crafted, cut, sharpened, like the old man's knife, like the entire visible scene. Is this not pop? No, we think. Knowing machines like we do, we don't want this. Floating high above? We don't want that. It's the perspective of modern times, the modern grind, the machine age blues, the cattle in the pen: Chaplin's *Modern Times* (1936), the remote camera looking down at the film's start, looking down on the sheep and scurrying, working men.

But was it always so? I think of Piet Mondrian's luminous last painting, *Broadway Boogie Woogie* (1943): "a resilient refugee's overhead, concrete view of Manhattan at night." This perspective, both present and absent, was central to the urban poetics of the *Seven Arts*, Louis Untermeyer's "A Side Street," say, where the poet also observes children observing the city. The poem finishes like this: they, like the poet, are "A part of life and yet apart from it." There's wisdom there.

When *Manhatta* was released, there was a real sense of urgency to redeem the city. Oppenheim looked to Los Angeles, while Frank looked to Chicago. New York City was a lost cause: "New York has *set*. New York is so perfectly Industrialism's flower, that no flower is left. Industrial disorder has its order. Industrial anarchy has its law." It is in this framework that *Manhatta* functions. How to reimagine, reuse the city? Cut, cut nice to make something new.

This is the film's first use of Whitman's verse: "City of the world / (for all races are here)" from "City of Ships." This is rewriting the city anew in the summer of 1921, the city of burning and terror and planes dropping bombs and closing borders. This is pop: space of unity and harmony—political, cultural, racial, aesthetic. But some lines get the cut. This is not the "mettlesome, mad, extravagant city!" of Whitman's Civil War poem.

This is a film of marble and iron, as the fifth intertitle reads ("Where our tall topt / marble and iron beauties / range on opposite sides" from "A Broadway Pageant"). Here we have contrast—in scale and speed—that the film ("our" film, "our" eyes) must navigate. But not just contrast. Here are principles of balance, order, and restraint by which the film rebuilds and rewrites the city. And so, we look on, as the city is reconfigured into organic patterns and even framed by classical arches.

What bothers critics so much about the film is precisely this: this order, this slowness, this feeling that everything is seen increasingly from afar, as the film's final shot of the sun makes clear. We start with the feeling of a floating approach. A tug neatly bisects the camera's own nearly imperceptible panning. Things bisect and perhaps you're in a painting by Mondrian; two shots later a long shot of the Brooklyn Bridge. A truck forms a speck slowly moving across the screen.

But then here they come. The approach of the ferry, one of only two head-on encounters in the film. This is old school admittedly, a preference of the *Seven Arts* for "a continuous composition, the figures moving into new harmonies as dancers move." It's the longest-held shot so far in the film. The ferry approaches, issues forth, a kind of finale. The crowd itself appears to shape-shift into an organic entity, like a surging flood of water. Is this effacement or a dream of a new pop order, where all races become Whitman's *En-Masse*?

That's an unpopular opinion, especially nowadays, and with good reason. The film repeats this sense of human morphing and diffusion, an increasingly unregimented crowd flowing against the geometry of a cemetery and the enormous windows of Wall Street. Should we think of Siegfried Kracauer's "mass ornament," should we find this worrisome, flat as a Busby Berkeley musical?

No. Doing so denies the complexity and contradictions of the artists connected to the *Seven Arts*, contributors like Randolph Bourne, for example, who celebrated pluralism, and what they brought, which was a lot, to our feeling for pop.

To understand the film's unique perspectives, its balance of order and chaos, its aspirations, turn to a contemporary source—Frank's *Our America*. In that pop critical work of 1919, Frank, like Kracauer, critiques the mass in the regimented city, linking its conformity to the skyscrapers that frame the "iron world": "Underneath, walks the multitude: colorless, cowed, the abject creature of its creation." But Frank also holds out another possibility, a "higher" vision, as it were, which is, in short, *Manhatta*: "The multitude has better powers. Can it not build higher than these buildings?"

The film is about that: building higher. The second section of intertitles (intertitles 4–9), beginning with "The building of cities" (from "A Song for Occupations") and concluding with "Shapes of the bridges, / vast frameworks, girders, arches" (from "Song of the Broad-Axe"), undertakes the work, constructing on screen something higher, something taller, "Mannahatta."

Strand and Sheeler, as well as Frank and even most New Yorkers, knew what this dream could look like. It looked like the past. Skyscrapers were creating ravines out of city streets, and soon it became popular to describe New Yorkers as "Cliff Dwellers." This drew upon a pop fascination with tribes of the Southwest that once built their dwellings high up on desert cliffs. Here again is Frank, thinking of the cinema, thinking of new ways of contemplation and engagement:

> *They built houses of several stories against the cliffs. They hollowed out great* kivas*—the silent places where they sought the Truth in meditation.*

And of the contemporary dwellings of the "Pueblo Indian":

> *The upper walls are reached by ladders that stand against the adobe flanks and rise from the many roofs to the roofs above. Here, at the sun's setting, the men sit on the highest summit of their building, wrapped in white sheets, and greet the night.*

Just like they cut up a new Whitman to learn film's direction, just as borders closed about them and they were giving up on Manhattan, a painter and a photographer, Sheeler and Strand, rebuilt the city (and film) cinematically, poetically, offering moviegoers another *kiva,* another summit on which to perch and "greet the night."

This film has no real drama, and its middle sequence reminds you of a director who has no idea what he's doing, Warhol, pointing a camera at a building at night and simply saying, "Look." The moment goes like this: *Manhatta* looks out to the bay, but finally culminates in a view of a pyramid-topped building in the foreground and another skyscraper nearly completed in the background. The film is halfway complete; halfway, too, the labor of the myth-building process, the making, the poetry. The film's very center captures both present and past, labor and artifact. In more stunning design, the filmmakers balance this directly before and after with two nearly identical shots of columns. We look through them. The columns repeat. The shots repeat, give structure, form. We look through them. Why? It's how and where the directors secure a vision of past and future, of close up and far away, of marble and iron.

This is Frank's *kiva,* a new way of seeing, a contemplative screen, a "silent place" to seek "the Truth in meditation." Like the peering eyes of the Brooklyn Bridge, like a door you look through, this is the cinematic screen for the artists of the *Seven Arts.* The columns provide a bifocal lens. Here, look!, the material and the spiritual coexist.

Here. Look! It's 1921. It's today.

Here. Look! The epic is immanent in the everyday.

Manhattan Resurrected

Post-9/11 Cinema

How do we heal the wound of film?

How do we use the machine that causes trauma to build something new? To recover?

In short, what are movies good for—if not to keep us in the dark with strangers and let us emerge as ones who share now a common dream?

In short, what are movies good for—if not magic?

PART 1. TWO FILMS: *HUGO* AND *EXTREMELY LOUD & INCREDIBLY CLOSE*

Something is falling.
From a window.
Is it a bird? Is it a plane?
It's a man. It's a man.

Is it a dream?

When Martin Scorsese's *Hugo* and Stephen Daldry's *Extremely Loud & Incredibly Close* opened within weeks of each other in the winter of 2011, even a journal of record as uncritical as *Entertainment Weekly* was moved to note: "Extremely Similar, Incredibly Close?"

The films take place in different centuries, but "Their plots have some weird resemblances." Both films feature boys in possession of a mysterious key, and the boys attempt to unlock messages left by dead fathers.

What to make of this odd mirroring? This strange repetition? These twins?

They came into the world around the tenth anniversary of the 9/11 attacks.

And what's it mean when things mirror each other but don't?

The magazine, alas, is silent on the matter, flummoxed no doubt by two films that, on second thought, hardly seem similar at all. Originally scheduled for release on the tenth anniversary of 9/11, Daldry's film, based on Jonathan Safran Foer's 2005 novel about a boy on a quest in post-9/11 New York, was conceived from the start as a cinematic memorial. Doing commemorative work of a very different kind, Scorsese's historical fantasy is based on Brian Selznick's 2007 graphic novel about a boy recovering the work of early filmmaker Georges Méliès. *Hugo* takes place in early twentieth-century Paris, in a train station and city that both feel, especially in 3-D, outside of ordinary time.

Given the divisive nature of every attempt to memorialize 9/11—from architecture (the National September 11 Memorial and Museum) to sculpture (Eric Fischl's *Tumbling Woman*)—it's tempting to tackle this case study in pop culture and repetition. Did Hollywood's effort to adapt Foer's literary-minded, intimate memorial come with its own secret twin, its own double? A Twin Tower? A movie-minded doppel? A split in our dream of what we want from pop?

Did Hollywood try twice, without even knowing it? Was *Extremely Loud & Incredibly Close* shadowed by a film committed to the extremely far away, a long view of pop that is more enduring, more sustaining (in the long run)? In memorializing 9/11, we are haunted, I think. Can pop give us distance? We want that, need that, even when apart, anxious, fractured, distant. Like today. Isn't this what Michiko Kakutani refers to as the "historical perspective" artists need "to grapple convincingly" with "the events of that day"?

Do we want to grapple?

Call it old school. Call it throwback. We need movies, even more than we need books, especially when the screen seems to cut us, terrify us. Scorsese understands this. Risk. Love. We need to see film again as if from a distance.

From extremely far away. We need distance, history, time. And then we can learn to look again.

When it comes to 9/11 tributes, Scorsese's *Hugo* is the more powerful.

Daldry's film is a cinematic memorial, but *Hugo* is a memorial for the cinema. Elegy. Homage.

Hugo grapples with that day's fearful specter of runaway machines. Machines that haunt a vulnerable city. Us. Through the lens of early cinema, *Hugo* returns us to the long ago, to the past, to what Marshall Berman liked to call the maelstrom of the city where we are under threat, where we are spellbound as well. Then feels like now. The film's historical perspective lands us in a recognizable post-9/11 cityscape. *Hugo* remembers that city, and what it means to be modern. Modernist. Memorial, elegy, homage. Remembers, gives distance. And in remembering that city, that time, and its fearsome (and magic) machines, the film reminds us who live after 9/11—who live today, and tomorrow, and the tomorrows that look like yesterday—how to live again.

Can we find a home in the maelstrom? You can.

You make its rhythms your own.

Scorsese's film says this: Our age's runaway machines include film itself. The civic technology was also an accomplice in the blockbuster design of the attacks, of course. This is why, for Scorsese, the train is a weapon in *Hugo*; why the Lumière symbol of the cinematic attraction, of film itself, gets weaponized in his Paris fantasy of 1890s–1930s. It is centrifugal, spiraling out of control, running off the rails. It must be harnessed, and film must be harnessed, to reestablish a new and different kind of unity.

Daldry, instead, pays tribute to more conventional modes of post-9/11 commemoration. The private, static, photographic. He builds for his character, Oskar, an insulated city, a fantasy city, the "Gotham wise-child genre." This city, as film critics complained, feels all too safe, private, hardly public at all.

Most significant, perhaps, is this: *Extremely Loud & Incredibly Close* gives us a city that has no place for the movies.

"Why not take a day off and watch a movie?" Oskar is asked this during his search. His response: No time. Nothing can get in the way. Scorsese, with *Hugo*, corrects that.

Another way to say that is this: *Extremely Loud & Incredibly Close* is a movie with hardly any shared civic space, hardly any room for pop. Scorsese, setting his film in a train station that is at once home, dance hall, and prison, corrects that, too.

Perhaps this lack is typical now. We as a culture are allergic to the shared vision, to any sense of public exposure, to anything not curated. *Bird Box*, perhaps, with its blinders on, lives in that space—pop in a viral age—and tries to find a way through: to a new shared space, where we all stream (dream) together. Daldry's film embodies this fear, this allergy. We feel there is a threat and maybe, surely, there is. But here's the problem, and it's not a small one: This inability to imagine civic space becomes an inability to engage meaningfully with public grieving, with what art can do.

Hugo, on the other hand, makes a simple claim for the redeeming civic function of film, and especially its commemorative function. Reviewers received it simply yet warmly at the time as the quintessential New York City director's "love letter" to the movies. And it was, in some ways. But maybe *Hugo* was also an understated gesture in a year of memorials. A commemorative act that went unheralded. Maybe the long view of the old school is what we need.

Among 9/11's ruins was the public faith in the healing power of cinema. That's what *Hugo* says, more or less. And that's a wound that only the cinema can address.

Part 2. The Same Pictures Over and Over

Let's remember, together, the cinema's fraught place among cultural first responders. Remember, for starters, that "the events of that day" included not only terror, but a sense that our spectator culture was to blame. That the simulacrum had finally come home to roost—that reality had become one of our "countless disaster movies," and yes, that was the immediate, if not unexpected pronouncement from Jean Baudrillard, while Slavoj Žižek argued that the terrorist act was committed "for the spectacular effect of it."

Of course, when the day's visual legacy and its terrifying effects are one and the same—"I lowered the volume until it was silent. / The same pictures over and over. / Planes going into buildings. / Bodies falling," as one of Foer's characters writes—a problem sets in (the problem that has dogged most artists responding to 9/11 from Foer to Fischl). How to touch such an event when the visual record is part of—really, the point of—the terror? This is not about accuracy, as Kakutani puts it, of "being eclipsed by the documentary testimony . . . still freshly seared" in the audience's mind. Rather, how "the events of that day" become a kind of visual stain spreading to everything, threatening to make every effort at commemoration yet another traumatic repetition.

Here is one critic's response to Michael Arad's "Reflecting Absence," the early designs for the 9/11 Memorial fountain: "In concept, they looked to me like an endless replay of the cascading curtain walls of the collapsing towers." Water. What has more of a traditional civic function? What is more human? What can we all point to and say, together, *I thirst*? That water simply *moves* now makes it unfit commemorative material.

Of course, that's not it, that's not it at all. The real issue here is water's new likeness—its motion, its repetition—to another cultural form hijacked on that day. Falling water looks now like a film replaying, an image repeating, a screen of sorts to the newly baptized, baptized in fire and into the culture of trauma.

For us there is no water.

At that moment, the skies were opened and something descended like a dove.

John the Baptist saw it. Was it a bird? A man? The Spirit of God?

Maybe he saw it. Maybe he didn't. He was pouring water over the Christ's head.

Part 3. Microhistories

Question: Why has grappling with and commemorating 9/11 been so hard? Why is it marked less by received forms and more by what Juan Suarez calls the "microhistory"? By narratives that avoid the shared story, the shared vision?

In part, because of the photograph: The photograph quickly assumed a new prominence, uniquely suited to capturing "particular individuals . . . without any claims to representativeness."

Remember (and it's hard to forget) "The Portraits of Grief" series from the *New York Times*? It was published as a book in the summer of 2002, its genesis a flood of "flyers identifying the missing" that papered the streets. As Nancy Miller traces in her essay on the portraits, the *Times* writers behind the volume considered their sketches in terms of specific visual media, calling them "snapshots," "vignettes," and thus "utterly democratic." There is, of course, a liberating street modernism in all of this. Small gestures, still lifes. We remember. But the vignette is also a well-rehearsed move in times of crisis, especially when we feel the city is threatening, is just too much, and we must escape.

The vignette was especially popular in the 1890s, the age of early cinema—a time of upheaval, an age of an exploding visual culture and unceasing movement. How to find shelter? Readers were offered solace by works like Brander Matthews's *Vignettes of Manhattan: Outlines in Local Color* (1894): "A dozen of them," Matthews notes in his dedication to native Manhattanite Theodore Roosevelt, "one for every month of the year, an urban calendar of times and seasons."

Sketches and snapshots, a book of vignettes, whether in the 1890s or 2002, reflect our search for order, our need to arrange, to stave off and arrest time. Create an urban calendar. This impulse, obviously, is all the more urgent in the face of a public realm pulsating to new rhythms, new technologies like film that both fascinated and horrified writers like Matthews, one of the nation's first to write about the cinema and its disorienting energies in his short fiction.

Can film heal fragmentation or does it only cause it? Matthews wondered about this in the 1890s. He was as ambivalent as Foer more than a century later. The flipside of the cinematic—what ties together 1890s and post-9/11 New York—is the comfort of the vignette, which frees us from the realm of pop. To dream of an arrested city, where nothing happens, where things just stop—this is the dream of a city made private, of private lives and ordered time, but this dream is just a dream. We know that now. We have lived it. This dream always gets shadowed by a strange cinematic double, one whose public, communal visions function as both threat and fantasy. This is how *Hugo* shadows and doubles the dream of Foer's work and Daldry's film, why it pushes us to reclaim our technology, which wounds, yes, but may bind and suture as well.

This kind of shadowing has been evident from the very start of the post-9/11 era; it's right there in the earliest cinematic memorial of sorts, Alain Brigand's *11'09"01* (2002), a series of cinematic vignettes, a calendar of sorts, a way of ordering time, with eleven shorts each eleven minutes, nine seconds, and one frame each. One outlier shadows these private vignettes, and it's come to receive the most attention: Alejandro González Iñárritu's "Mexico," originally called "nakedly exploitative" because of its "evocation and infliction of trauma" by one reviewer, and "an unremitting monstrosity" by another.

Built around brief flashes of the "Planes going into buildings. / Bodies falling" that Foer's character silently watches, the film appears, like falling water, to revel in motion, repetition. These are the qualities, remember, that exclude the medium from commemorative work. And, in a way, the film acknowledges this exclusion. It's mostly a film of a darkened screen. While this technique, accompanied by a soundscape of apparent chanting, news footage, and white noise no doubt points to the "shutting down of coherent vision," as one critic notes, it also gestures back to film history—indeed, all the way back to the 1890s and the tradition of titillating exhibition and showmanship that disoriented early writers like Matthews. This is elegy. This is homage.

You Will See This Man Take Flight!

The film historian Tom Gunning reminds us that early cinema offered presentation styles "that addressed and held the spectator, emphasizing the act of display." Stilled screens, confrontation: "See the still image spring to life! In just a moment," says the exhibitor pointing to the screen, "you will see this train take life!" A darkened screen also did the trick, as Iñárritu reminds us.

But why this gesture back to early cinema? Why this pop throwback, which has become more and more common post-9/11?

It's an attempt, I think, to recover a shared experience, to remember a sense of risk, as Scorsese has recently called it. You sit in the dark with others. That's what moviegoing is, remember? It's a feeling of public exposure at odds with the confines of the microhistory, the private memorial, the vignette, and the private machines of post-9/11 life.

This throwback gesture, this memory of pop and of film as public space, finds its symbol in the falling man, strangely enough. The photo made famous of a man falling, leaping from the North Tower, caught by Richard Drew in a position of strange transcendence. Do you remember?

"He departs from this Earth like an arrow," writes Tom Junod, and he's right. Like an arrow. He cuts. He is an unsmiling anti-vignette, an anti-portrait of grief—he violates legibility, he who puts us all at a loss, he who is, to Laura Frost, "a public death that is also anonymous."

We don't want him. We want vignettes. We want sentiments. But Iñárritu and *Hugo*, I think, want us to come to terms with film itself, want to return us to the source, to the medium's earliest iteration in shock and risk.

Might we find there, at the source of the wound, also a space of transcendence and healing?

As much is suggested by the opening sounds of Chamulas Indians chanting a prayer for the dead before Iñárritu's darkened screen. Is this a séance? What else can we do with our media? As Iñárritu's film puts it with a final question: "Does God's light guide us or blind us?"

It's a question that can also be addressed to the light of the cinematic machine. Was it designed to terrorize us? Might we not reimagine a technology capable of suturing us? This broken age?

If you know Foer's book, or have even picked up a copy and looked at its pages, then you must know where this is going. Iñárritu's return to early cinema is part of Foer's strategy as well. Even those who've not read the book know how it ends. You turn the pages and discover, look!, a reverse-order flipbook constructed by the novel's hero, nine-year-old Oskar Schell.

What does it show?

It shows, in just a moment, a series of photos . . . of a falling man now falling magically upwards. A sleight of hand, a dream worthy of early cinema's exhibitors. The Futurists talked of this, this kind of creative-destruction, the new power of film that could reverse every demolition into construction, every fall into flight.

But in Foer's gesture there's ambivalence, and in Daldry's film much more. Both make the public private, the moving becomes too still, too arrested. Dead, even. Daldry will turn the falling man into Oskar's father. The attraction gets tamed; there is no risk here. We erase the feeling of a public grief; we give it a name, a face, and ask that it no longer speak in its unknowable tongue.

We turn the pages. Here is but one more private portrait of grief. And, of course, look closer. The book's film is, in fact, not a film at all. Foer longs "for the still time of the photograph," it's been said; the falling man "is in exactly the same pose at every point in his ascent." This is not a pop reproduction. Everything is too safe. We don't believe, finally, that here we see flight; we don't believe, finally, that here we see film. We don't believe, finally.

Part 4. Adaptations

Here are a few strange reviews in the history of books and films.

Walter Kirn on Foer's novel: "With such a high-concept visual kicker" (referring to the flipbook visuals at the end), does it really even need a title—further, "Does it even need text?"

There was something, it seemed, about the end that was rather suspicious, something that erased discourse.

The film, on the other hand, seemed to lack visuals, was overrun with words. David Denby: "The sound of a hyper-articulate boy talking semi-nonsense becomes very hard to take."

If the book's text threatened to become superfluous, Daldry's film adaptation applied a reverse calculus. The result was the feeling that a cinematic opportunity had been missed, with the powers of the medium left untapped. Why did this strange film seem so uncomfortable with film itself? With communication?

Here's *Timeout*: "Less a film about communication, in the end, than one with its fingers in its ears."

This is a nod to the film's promotional material. Oskar covers his mouth with his hands—the failure of communication in the face of grief. There's the speechlessness of the Renter (Oskar's grandfather) and Oskar's own "pathos of over-cerebration." How to handle this complex problem? Daldry does it, oddly, through unceasing voiceover, giving, in the end, a barely glimpsed city skirting about the edges of the chattering film. But perhaps a private, chattering technology is not that strange at all. Sure, we dream of technology that connects us, that leads us beyond private things, to others. But isn't that just a dream from long ago?

❧

Twenty-First Century Machines: Or, Private Things

In Daldry's film, machines are private things that buffer you from a noisy, public, frenetic world. Foer's invention, in fact, is a character for the new age of inventions and apps, an inventor of fantasy tech—less a stream of consciousness than consciousness of the Stream. (On this stream, of course, everyone rows a private boat.) Hear Oskar chatter: "What about . . . / What about . . . / What about . . ." Call it the refrain for the age of the app. *I saw the best minds of my generation*: No. Here is a different kind of howl. How. And the book has barely started.

While the debt is hard to see, Oskar's most obvious literary ancestor is none other than that always inventing ad-man who makes his own urban odyssey while quietly grieving a lost son: James Joyce's Leopold Bloom. Bloom is a kind of reverse Oskar in more ways than one. The two together are a fair measure of pop and what's happened to it. They look the same, but they're not. Bloom's mind: public-oriented, responsive to the city's civic flow, at times considering public projects, at times innovating new ways to reach out and touch someone. "Good idea that." That's Bloom considering a rowboat that displays advertisements. "How can you own water really? . . . Because life is a stream. All kinds of places are good for ads." All kinds. And if you follow the stream of consciousness, and you're thinking of rowboats, then things pool into an inventive idea after a while. Here's one: "A transparent showcart with two smart girls inside writing letters. . . . I bet that would have caught on. . . . Everyone dying to know what she's writing." Revealing writing for all.

Pop art. On every page of *Ulysses*. Anonymous. What is she writing? To whom? Here is modernism's generous desire to type some letters on the urban script—make it, by turns, illegible, fragmented, fascinating, for all of us. All.

Oskar's efforts are different. Do we see ourselves in this? Our need to quiet that noise, to control, to be safe? His dream of invention: "What about a device that knew everyone you knew? So when an ambulance went down the street, a big sign on the roof could flash DON'T WORRY!" Oskar's desire is the dream of reducing exposure; it's a dream of legibility, but perhaps we should call it fragility. And being "safe" (the final word of the book) creates, in turn, a city made oddly private, divided. The civic space, it turns out, gets muffled by the very technology designed to connect people.

To contrast the two is to measure pop, the feeling of exposure to others, which is what pop has provided us all along. *How does it feel?* If it feels like there is risk, that's OK, pop says, or once did.

Foer wants that, too, but exposure is fraught. His machines are private, like the baby monitor Oskar and his grandmother use to communicate.

On the Baby Monitor in Art and Literature

A history of the baby monitor in the arts surely needs telling, especially in an age when parents are helicopters. That history would at the very least include this:

1. Its design by Isamu Noguchi, who studied under Brancusi, and developed something in the 1930s that looked like a bird in space, a lovely Bakelite abstraction (this, after Lucky Lindy's baby was taken—"the biggest story," said Mencken, "since the Resurrection"). His "Radio Nurse" for Zenith never quite worked as it might or ought, but it was displayed at the Whitney. A form that sat in bedrooms, no doubt, crying like a Dos Passos novel, picking up the babel of babies—and more—everywhere on the block.

2. Near the end, this history includes Foer, and his literary style, a listening in that threatens to muffle everything. A prose of panic. "What about little microphones? What if everyone swallowed them, and they played the sounds of our hearts through little speakers . . . ?" We need hardly to imagine.

The public gets effaced, in other words. Tamed, made private. The self expands its domain. In some sense, it's what our faces do, don't they?, when they intrude, invade what is otherwise a shared space. To be fair to Foer, he knows this, and negotiates these feelings in a complex text where portraits are taken of the back of people's heads. But Daldry's film is different.

History, in the film, is a setting for a selfie. How it works:

1. Oskar is on a quest. There once was a Sixth Borough, the evidence of which may be found, according to his father's bedtime story, in the park that was once a part of the lost borough. The borough floated away, but not before New Yorkers dragged Central Park into Manhattan, the father explains early on. Central Park, in this telling, is a kind of pop palimpsest, a shared space, a place to dig into the lives of others.
2. The film is not comfortable with this. See Oskar with his metal detector, detecting. And then a curious cut. Oskar goes from digging in Central Park to digging in another box that the viewer may very well think is part of his search. No, the box, it turns out, contains his grandfather's camera and his grandmother's old home movies, old media forms that Oskar handles as if strange relics from some lost age: "Where's this from?" (camera), "What's this?" (film reel).

Why do this? It's Daldry reflecting on the role of visual media as a means of recovering and remembering. But we are now in the private space, where film will be tamed, made private. Watch:

3. The night before the attacks, Oskar screens the film on an old projector and asks his father, "Do you know what your father looked like?" To which Dad answers, "No, not a clue." Speaking while the grandmother's film of the ruined streets of Dresden *is projected upon him*, the father in a quite literal way enters the film screening, the home movie. Dad is an emblem of the photographic, or at least what we want from photography. The face. Dad replaces the faceless father, just as he will replace the falling man. The result is odd. The desolate, totally empty Dresden streets of the grandmother's film get peopled with family. It's a statement about Foer's work in general, maybe, but also about how Daldry wants to domesticate the cinematic machine and the city. Like Oskar, the director believes in private machines. He desires to shield us from both movies and the city. Daldry does just that by putting the paternal camera in Oskar's hands, and turning the film over to the portrait-making power of photography.

Portraits of grief. Vignettes.

The film turns away from film. Daldry's Oskar doesn't make a proto-film of the falling man. Instead, the film ends with his mother finding his scrapbook drawings, the falling man now a trick in a children's book. And this softened ending is a kind of bookend to the film's opening, where we see an extreme close-up of the falling man. Abstraction is what happens when you're extremely close to things, but sometimes it's facile, sentimental. At first glance, the clothed body appears to be more or less floating, slowly moving in two directions at once and thus curiously suspended. And this is in keeping with a film that, it turns out, bears the imprint of photography's history in other, more allusive ways.

At a key moment in the film, Oskar realizes at once that the Renter is his grandfather and decides to share with him his father's final phone messages. The faceless man gets a face, and private grief is shared. This, you'll remember, is the film's calculus. The scene occurs before a heavily scratched, bright red factory wall. Oskar, on the right side of the frame, touches the wall as his grandfather stands facing him on the far left. Pulled as a still for the film's DVD cover, the image bears striking resemblance to another famous photograph of a boy touching a scratched wall, Henri Cartier-Bresson's *Valencia, Spain* (1933). One of the pioneers of photojournalism, Cartier-Bresson pivots on what he famously called the "decisive moment" that, in the words of Peter Galassi, transforms the boy next to the wall "into a figure of rapture." Is he blind? Is there something above him?

Look at the puddle jumper in Cartier-Bresson's *Behind the Gare St. Lazare* (1932): Lazarus leaping Lethe. (Watch the dead rise.) Look at the aesthetic of suspension in *Valencia, Spain*. The arrested, transfigured moment of the photojournalistic vignette is an anti-gravitational dream—this has been central to 9/11 commemorative efforts, which keep the falling bodies "still in the realm of the air" (from Wisława Szymborska's poem "A Photograph from Sept. 11"). Foer's work, too, is deeply invested in this. Oskar's obsession with the falling man derives originally from his father's bedtime story. In it a long jumper completes a leap between the city and the Sixth Borough each year. The jump, the father explains, makes every New Yorker "feel capable of flight," but then he qualifies: "Or maybe 'suspension' is the better word," since what mattered was not the motion but "how he stayed between them for so long."

This all gets reflected in Oskar's oddly arrested flipbook, and in Foer's novel, a fantasy in exorcising movement, a fantasy which points back to film's source in Eadweard Muybridge's photography. This photography—this vision—illustrates the book, revises the trauma.

Why?

Because real movement implies destruction, both in the novel and the film.

This is, after all, how Foer speaks of the novelist's job. Books arrest movement. Freeze. That's why Oskar's flipbook seeks to prevent the drift, the crumbling, the terror. For Foer, the old-fashioned technology on which we must rely, ultimately, is the novel, because what it arrests is the private voice, making it heard across time and space. As Foer has explained in interviews, novels "show us that conversations are possible across distances." And that, of course, is the ending of the father's story: "On a frozen shelf, in a closet frozen shut, is a can with a voice in it," a voice that says, "I love you."

There is, in the film, little disaster. In the book the Sixth Borough floated away from the city and "The eight bridges between Manhattan and the Sixth Borough strained and finally crumbled. . . . The phone and electrical lines snapped, requiring Sixth Boroughers to revert to old-fashioned technologies, most of which resembled children's toys." Daldry leaves much of this out. Left out are images of a vulnerable New York, its tunnels and bridges collapsing. Suppressed, both details exert an odd pressure on the film. They are there in the film's final frame.

See Oskar frozen in, of course, midflight, having mastered his fear of a terrifying, noisy, unsafe machine: the playground swing. The swing is an apt symbol to end a film that avoids grappling with the real fears of an age wary of its runaway machines and its devastated cities. It is in flight from all of that.

A final word on Oskar.

We dream of freezing the city. But we know we ultimately can't. (Frozen cities are dying cities, plague cities. We know that now.)

In one of the more powerful portraits of the twenty-first century child, the child of 9/11 (like Rue of HBO's *Euphoria* [2019], born three days after the attacks), we find Oskar alone in the bathroom. Raiding the medicine cabinet? Cutting? No, not exactly.

What is he doing?

He has his fingers in his ears. He's in a bathroom alone, and he's trying not to listen to the slow drip of a faucet, which in startling close-up takes on the scale of a fountain.

A fountain?

Water remembers. Water moves. This is pop. This is memorial. This is elegy. Everywhere you look. The surfaces of things turn and turn into something else. This is the frozen city melting, or perhaps mourning, but what's the difference, really?

The water drips, things change, are beyond the control of the technocratic age, and this indeed is terrifying to us curators, we who curate our lives, our grief, we who cut, we who are relentlessly private, who look out and see no public rituals worthy of our grief. Belief.

In the film the water turns, but just for a moment, into an abstracted falling body, a moment worthy of the German Expressionist tradition, like something from F. W. Murnau's

The Last Laugh (1924). It's a lovely, stirring moment. It is true to Foer at his best, and at his best he's remarkable. But the film turns away. We turn away. Much better, the chattering film suggests, as have critics of 9/11 memorializing efforts, to look away, to suspend motion, to offer moviegoers cold comfort as Daldry did in the winter of 2011.

Extremely Loud is actually frozen beneath its autumnal surface. *Hugo*, on the other hand, uses snow and a wintry landscape as a complex symbol like Joyce does at the end of "The Dead." Here is the temptation to retreat from history ten years after 9/11, which Scorsese takes head on.

I've read that Scorsese challenged his 3-D designers to make the swirling snow even more dramatic at the film's opening, which cost a small fortune. Why? To be true to Selznick's text, where the snow quiets a noisy, kinetic world. At least it does for Georges Méliès, the one-time early cinema pioneer (now broken-down toy store owner) whose films, legacy, and life will be recovered and restored in 1930s Paris thanks to the orphaned hero of Selznick's historical fantasy, Hugo Cabret. Pop must come back to life. Méliès is retreating from history. (Méliès is our figure for pop, of course.) We must save him. Save pop, save Méliès—who in the end becomes Hugo's godfather, his pop-pop.

1. The Plot: The two meet early in the graphic novel, as Hugo attempts to recover his dead father's book of mechanical drawings from Méliès. He follows the old man home. The drawings are of an automaton—the tale's "mechanical man," which the boy must get to work. Getting back his father's book opens the tale. Scorsese deftly makes it into a flipbook, reversing Foer, in a way. Its forward motion turns the automaton's head to confront the viewer. Us. This is an emblem of the cinematic attraction that the film will take head-on. Scorsese doesn't want you to look away.
2. Hugo is eager to fix—to put into motion—the mechanical man in order to receive a message from

> his father. When he follows Méliès home, Hugo is chided by the broken man: "'Stop clicking the street with your heels.' Then, quietly, he said to himself, 'I hope the snow covers everything so all the footsteps are silenced, and the whole city can be at peace.'"

Méliès wants to arrest motion, to freeze the city into a deathly sleep. That's clear in Selznick, and Scorsese picks up on that. It's precisely what his film will not allow. It's what Scorsese will not allow. It's what we must not allow. Film must work again, which means Hugo must make the mechanical man work again. To do so is to reveal Méliès's past, our connection to it, and, of course, to machines. Machines must move, and we must move with them and through them, which in this film means we must learn again how to dance.

The Civic Dance and the City

Hugo, like other post-9/11 works, reimagines the city—the city that threatens to fall asleep, the city that threatens to be frozen, arrested. Selznick's tale relies on film history for inspiration on this point: "Hugo remembered another movie he and his father had seen a few years earlier, where time stops in all of Paris, and everyone is frozen in their tracks. But the night watchman of the Eiffel Tower, and some passengers who land in an airplane, are able to move around the silent city. What would that be like? [But] time won't stop."

Scorsese's swirling, floating, and rapidly descending opening sequence is a complex rejoinder to these fantasies. A ticking clock gear dissolves into the unceasing traffic of the city, as a floating camera plunges into the busy train station.

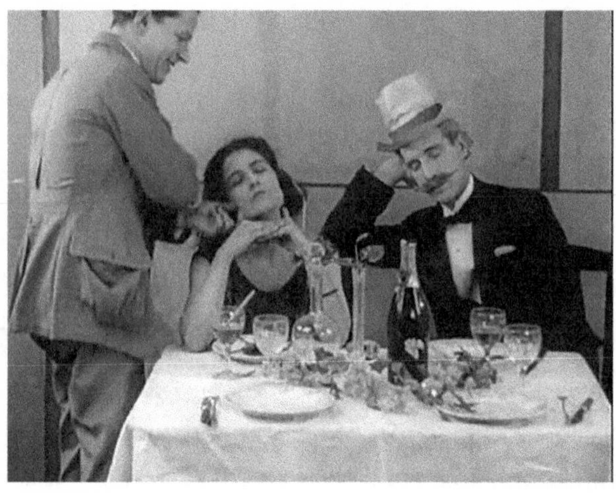

Finally, we find Hugo's face peering from behind the train station's clock. And so we begin.

This start, in fact, is a repetition and reversal of René Clair's *Paris Asleep* (1924), the film that Hugo recalls watching with his father: Scorsese establishes that his film will be about a city very much awake, very much unfrozen. His city moves in a kind of energized civic dance that his main characters must join. Hugo, Méliès, and even the wounded World War I veteran, the Station Inspector—each is arrested with grief, haunted by trauma. (The first shot of Ben Kingsley's Méliès shows him completely still at his toy store counter, where he often sleeps, as if one of Clair's characters. Meanwhile, see the camera focus on the Inspector's rusty knee brace, which continually locks throughout the film.)

Bodies are meant to move and have their being here. So are machines. The idea of a civic dance, it turns out, is actually a sophisticated technological conceit in Scorsese's opening. Here he deviates far from his rather functional source material in Selznick, and thank modernism for that. For this is a modernist adaptation. The sweeping camera revels in the coordinated movements of café dancers—in public energies, in public spaces. Look! None other than James Joyce looks on. Scorsese's historical gesture situates the film in a fertile creative period following the mechanized wars of World War I. War, of course, is a specter of violence and communal breakdown all but absent from Selznick's work.

Not here. The film is set a decade after that war, just as *Hugo* gets released a decade after the 9/11 attacks. Scorsese is tactical. This historical perspective lets him reclaim art's public revelry and civic-mindedness in a way that modernists like Joyce once did. This is, obviously, a position at odds with Foer's private machines and sheltered spaces.

If that wounded era was ready to reclaim the magical powers of Méliès's early cinema—to reclaim technology, especially film's centripetal, binding, suturing, civic powers—Scorsese asks us: Might not our own? What are we waiting for?

If you want to reclaim the cinema, however, you have to come to terms with why we must. This is where Scorsese's film differs from Daldry's most. Scorsese's darker fantasy is a far cry from what's been called *Extremely Loud*'s "false uplift" and "cloying sentimentalization of collective memory." This, again, is a modernist adaptation one hundred years on. The opening close-up on gears and wheels announces that "the machine [is] the leading character, the leading actor" in *Hugo*, to quote the French painter Fernand Léger's enthusiastic response to Abel Gance's *The Wheel* (1923). Scorsese's turning wheel keeps turning us back to Gance's film, most famous for its montage train crash that smashes its way through *Hugo*.

We must remember how artists like Léger struggled to accommodate and articulate the machine's place in art. He argued that *The Wheel* was liberating because it "crushes and eliminates the human object, reduces its interest, pulverizes it." Léger would go on to collaborate on *Ballet Mécanique* (1924), part of the "modernist tradition of using dance . . . to figure the motion of machinic modernity." Scorsese is no cubist; nevertheless, he draws on this modernist tradition in an opening sequence that connects spinning gears, turning traffic, and twirling dancers into a thing of public beauty, a moving mural for all to see. But with a difference. Scorsese knows, at any moment, things can fall apart. And in this difference—this risk, vulnerability, and human touch—is pop. Scorsese is no Futurist. Léger's idealism, his brand of Futurist frenzy, is not Scorsese's, who knows, at this late date, that gears sometimes can spin out of control, and the dancers, even the dancers in all their beauty, are not safe.

His film does not flinch from the feeling that we're living in a crash, in other words. That life after 9/11 has changed, changed utterly, but we've endured before and art can help us again. This is why Scorsese makes the terrifying 1895 Montparnasse train crash a centerpiece even more than his source material does, and further, why the nightmare sequence of a runaway train destroying the station turns into yet another nightmare—Hugo's transformation into a machine. They are one and the same.

In weaponizing the Lumière symbol of the cinematic attraction, Scorsese gives us not a plane but a train going into, through, and out of the window of a building. Here is the terror of 9/11 after the fact, and before it. This is a frightening reversal of Scorsese's careful opening, the entrance into the station and the close-up on Hugo's face. It's almost as if the director wants us to feel how easily things fall apart. And how beauty, in the end, is no protection.

We get it. We know well the machine's capacity to terrorize. We understand. We've seen true terror, what it rips apart. Not a nation, really. Or not just. Rather, it's a violation of something more fragile—a civic space, the dance space, the moving, communal city, where everything always is dancing. This leaves the individual alone, arrested, wounded by the machine.

(As Hugo's legs turn into metal in his second nightmare, you are put in mind of another mechanized body, the Station Inspector's. And perhaps your own.)

But this is not the end. Chaos is not film's final legacy, its last word, as long as we remember its original design: "The sole purpose" of such machines, Selznick writes of the automaton (whose leftover parts Méliès uses to build his first camera), "was to fill people with wonder."

I wonder. Do we think that still?

Do we look upon the world, like a child, and wonder? There is your mother floating next to a tree. (You're at the movies. You're watching *The Tree of Life,* another film from 9/11's ten-year memorial.)

Without wonder, without that memory—lacking historical perspective, in other words—we see only terror. Everything is fragmentation precisely because we are too "incredibly close" to it all, to use Foer's phrase. In Selznick, "up close" the city "just seemed noisy and disconnected" to Hugo; and when the mechanical man finally writes, it first looks like "random, disconnected markings."

But it's not so.

Look again. From its start film has connected us, even protected us, by sharing in our dreams and our wounded state. We are Etienne, the one-eyed character in Selznick's book. He is a figure for Méliès's one-eyed Man in the Moon, their shared wounding a symbol of Etienne's destiny to be a film director ("Having an eye patch actually makes it easier to look through a camera").

Look again. Trains crash, but Scorsese places you back in history, reinvests it all with a civic spirit, a communal spirit. These are not just "the same pictures over and over" that haunt Foer's frozen world. We look again. We are renewed.

Look again. See Méliès first experience Lumière's on-coming train in its original fairground context, where startled spectators soon turn joyful. We look again. We are renewed.

But we would much rather arrest movement. Turn away and in turning leave behind the cinematic machine, its shared public space.

But do we need another portrait of grief?

Are we not too close to it all?

Doesn't so much seem fragmented, disconnected?

Hugo reminds me—us—of what was lost.

(I look up. I search for the long view. I look up—from my phone, a GIF, like an early cinema loop. Grant me pop, grant me the long view. Because up close all I know are fragments. And maybe that's all there is, random, disconnected markings. Maybe. But what do I know? Perhaps you wait for me. Perhaps I wait for you, like Whitman beneath the sole of your shoe. Like Whitman who waits in the shit and the snow. Perhaps. You need to look. A different point of view. Too close, much too close to it all. Perhaps it takes a different point of view. Look up.

Look.)

5

Remnants, Scraps, Waste

Pop's Postscript

After Cohen

Thing about "Hallelujah": like something from Eliot, from Pound but whittled down. A bird in space. Brancusi. Line for line's sake.

~~Every line a surrender. Teaches you love. Writing, like~~ love, is not a victory march.

Quod scripsi, scripsi. INRI. I'm nailed right in.

Surrender. Surrender. Did I ever? Never have I ever. Leonard's song 80 verses long.

Cut it all. Love. Teach me how. What is left when most everything is gone?

He made it ugly; put it all to a Casio track. Leonard says, your turn. You sing along. These are the remains. The ashes.

Bring it all back home.

Eliot and Pound in a captain's tower.

Gives you a poem, says what do you think? Red ink.

Above the antique mantel was displayed
~~*In pigment, but so lively, you had thought*~~
(As though) a window gave upon the sylvan scene
The change of Philomel

Bird on a wire.

Winter kept us warm, covering
Earth in ~~forgetful~~ snow (Ezra, are you sure?)

You can't take everything away. That's what Pound's edits teach us.

Forgetful snow.

The cruellest month.

Dull roots.

Spring rain.

A little life.

A little life.

A little life.

After Carson

President elected. We felt cheated. Cohen had died.
    Poets tweeted

gyre wide af

Yeats's "The Second Coming."
Jesus, just say when. At the end.

The falcon cannot hear the falconer.
The auction cannot hear the auctioneer.

The nurse cannot hear.
The doctor cannot hear.
No. Nothing.
Me too?

All fall she read Anne Carson's *The Beauty of the Husband.*
Said you should read women more.

I feel I am turning into Emily Brontë
my lonely life around me like a moor

After Donne

Thing is how everything wants to be something else.
Bread ~~a body~~
Poem ~~prose~~
Word ~~made flesh~~
Piggy ~~toes~~

Contract Thine immensity, and shut Thyself within Syllables, and accept a Name from us.

God. He just wants to be loved.
God had skin. The flea bites you. The flea bites me.
Three bloods make the flea the Trinity.

Triads.

No sin, nor shame, nor loss of maidenhead

Good way to start.

Mark but this flea, and mark in this, how little that which thou deniest me is;

A little life.

After Kondo

Or like how a poem wants to be a painting.

> *For over a year I have been trying to make a poem of a very beautiful thing,*

wrote Pound.

> *Then only the other night, wondering how I should tell the adventure, it struck me that in Japan one might make a very little poem which would be translated as follows:*

Do these mom jeans spark joy?

Marie Kondo. A couple in a condo. They sing a cover of "Hallelujah."

> *I do not mean I found the words. But there came an equation not in speech, but in little splotches of color.*

The apparition of these faces in the crowd

Different versions of the same thing. Writing is about putting them all in there.

After Joyce

Or like a word wants to be a different word.

Come
To me, says Mary.

The quaker librarian. Quaking.

Blue-robed, white under, come to me. Mary always off to the side a bit. But sometimes the cross is, too.

Put the x back in xmas.

A bird held its flight, a swift pure cry, soar silver orb it leaped serene.

Joyce was maybe dreaming of Brancusi.

The endlessnessness.

I always liked that.
Repeat after me.

Endlessnessness

Endlessnessnessness

After Warhola

And it never stops like how a painting of one thing is actually another thing.

And a person another person.

Like Warhol who was Warhola who never had the words who barely ever wrote anything. He let his mother write the titles and kept her mistakes because who cares no editing.

Leave it all, keep it all. Don't be burdened.

25 Cats Name Sam and One Blue Pussy

Mom alled his book that. He kept it. Named. My mother name me.

My mother gave me a face but I pick my own nose.

First painting.

A colostomy bag, a pantry full of soup. She brought me this song.

Woman gave me soup and shelter. Died without a whisper.

Andy Andy Andy

And he did everything in memory of her.

do this in memory
a painting is not a painting is a mother
not a mother a wife not a wife a wife not a wife a wife
        not a wife twenty-five wives
how many soup cans did he paint
thirty-two
his mother a wife a mother a wife an artist
a mother a wife and more and more
how many of her were there
thirty-two
more than that
that's how many

Byzantine
Byzantine icons
His soup cans   eat this in memory of me

Her first child dead in her arms
A little girl
Julia
Warhola
Rather die with your child
Pieta
In a village in Slovakia
Mom and pop

A colostomy bag
Insides on her outsides   found that she was already dead
The man who saw it has given testimony, and his testimony is true I guess
These things happened so that the scripture would be fulfilled more or less
Not one of her bones will be broken
He knows that he tells the truth, and he testifies so that you also may believe
He knows that he tells the truth, and he testifies so that you also may believe
He knows that he tells the truth, and he testifies so that you also may assume

They pierced her side with a spear, bringing a sudden flow

Cream of mushroom

~~*(I John saw these things and heard them.)*~~
~~*(I John saw these things and heard them.)*~~
~~*(I John saw these things and heard them.)*~~

More!

Notes on Words, Images, Ideas

On things that don't repeat

The photograph *Andy Warhol and his mother, Julia Warhola* (1958) is, in fact, really only half the picture. If you want to see the other half, you'll have to wait for it. Or go and find it. I'll wait. The work is an early one by Duane Michals and provides a quiet introduction of sorts to so much of what follows in this book. I am grateful for his work, which inspired my own. What photos can't do; what they can do; motion, repetition, limits (and excess, too), Marcel Duchamp and Jonathan Safran Foer: All of it is there in Michals. He photographed Duchamp through the artist's apartment window in 1964. They were neighbors. Duchamp lived on tenth street. "I lived on ninth street," Michals writes in cursive hand on that photo, as he does on so many. ("The photographic shot is one of my sketch pads," says Henri Cartier-Bresson. Michals actually makes that come true. Scribbles. Crosses out. Actually writes *Look. See for yourself!* on a photo called "This Photograph Is My Proof." Proof. There's never enough. Look that up, too.) What was Duchamp building in there? A something that was secret, no doubt, and the glass between you and him in Michals's photo makes you feel it. Something of that secret ends Section One of this book.

Maybe go read it? And it's wise, perhaps, to return to Michals, too, after getting (too) incredibly close to things with Foer later on. Foer is haunted by what words can't do; Michals, by what they can do. ("My writing [on my photos] grew out of frustration with my photography.") Getting incredibly close is not the only way, and his twin photographs of Warhol and Julia prove it, offering here, the smiling boy, a bit blurred, but then another photo lets you reconstruct the scene, mother, and son. Your knowledge is incomplete, always incomplete. ("I never believed a photograph is worth a thousand words.") What's that other view of mother and son hold? Here's a hint: it doesn't repeat but it looks like it does. There's always more, in other words. You're both near and far. Smiles turn. (Andy's less nice.) You never step into the same river twice. Speaking of Warhol and the photographer's own work (his photographs are called "fictionettes" and "prose portraits"), Michals says, "You can't capture someone, per se. How could you?" I agree. Keep on, keepin' on. He's from Pittsburgh, too.

On revelation

The first essay, "Mother Cuts Flowers," makes a collage (or, like Julia, scissors something new) out of two short passages from Victor Bockris's biography of Warhol, and pays loving homage to Wayne Koestenbaum's A+ style in his *Warhol,* where, among other things, the poet-critic's rhapsodies on Julia's colostomy ensorcelled me. The best thing that can be said, perhaps, about a book like his is this: It made me see me in the artist, my childhood a time when every cut, do you remember?, turns you into a blade (or a blade of grass). I spent much time in speech class, hardly gradgrindian hard times, and there I spoke of a Suzanne of whom so many have spoken before; a girl who takes you down to a place by the water; told to repeat who she was and what she did. *She sells seashells by the seashore*: my bodily delay turning the procedural into a kind of ritual or something more, which isn't strange when you think about Joyce's Gerty MacDowell in "Nausicaa," little girl lost, limping, lustfully, liminally about, a head full of ads, pulp, head full of doubt like that kid in The Avett Brothers song ("this song inspired me not to kill myself," the top listener comment on YouTube. Go check it out. And the band Suicide on YouTube? "Suicide makes me want to keep living." Dream, baby, dream. Art can do that, it's done that for me; it creates for you a room, and in it there is no place that you are not seen. That's Rilke. Go check him out, too.) My tongue, to get back to it, was beyond my control like Andy and his early fits, the boy plagued by St. Vitus's dance, Vitus the patron saint of artists and entertainers, Vitus the martyr often depicted in a cauldron like he's jumped into a bowl of soup. Maybe that's a stretch but we forget how pop once oriented us, connected us not just in space but across time, too, like Muhammad Ali as St. Sebastian (*Esquire,* April 1968), pierced for our sins, icon for the iconoclastic. (Or Warhol, drowning in a giant soup can on the cover of the same magazine a year later. Vitus, indeed.)

Maybe it's a stretch, but my tongue was elastic. My speech turned me on to how *hoc est corpus* becomes *hocus pocus,* the old communion rite mispronounced, denounced, renounced. My cup I drank from as a kid had a picture of a crucified body with arms thrown wide. *Jesus loves you this much.* I thought that was a stretch. But who knows? What I do know is this: Children gathered around to hear me say consonants, vowels, like a priest or a heretic, like someone possessed or dispossessed. Language was a kind of inheritance I somehow missed, or maybe they did. Hard to tell. Still, they made me feel the difference. *They would gather around.* And, God, they would howl. The thing is, reader, it was wonderful. I thought it was. Just consonants and vowels and they would howl, laugh, fight for air. Was I purifying the language of the tribe? Like Mallarmé? Eliot? Pound? Hardly. I mean, that wasn't really the vibe. Not like they were handing out medals. Eliot and Pound, of course, took to hating on poor Henri Bergson who said becoming things, that we were things becoming, changing, ever evolving. "Slither" and "welter" (Pound concluded); took to parroting T. E. Hulme; traveling in, as Louis Menand says, "terrible fellowship." Some of this you must know already; and Eliot, can you see him?, haunted by dead poets, by Yeats and Poe, contemplates poetry and pop as bombs drop about him, writing "Little Gidding" in his head; the poet as air raid warden, listening for sirens (real sirens), wondering how to "use the speech which he finds about him," how to bind, to suture, to connect. "Emotion and feeling, then, are best expressed in the common language." Eliot, like Berryman, was wondering how to be an actual human being. And perhaps you see them fighting in the captain's tower, that often derided Dylan line from "Desolation Row"; but it rings truer if we see the captain dead, or close to it, Whitman nursing what still could be healed, Ginsberg shouldering the wheel. What were they fighting for, if not some common tongue? But how uncommon it is!, is all I guess I'm trying to say; how it slithers beyond your control, reproducing, marring, making everything new because of an absolute inability to do what it's told, like Andy, with Gerard Malanga, pushing the paint through, silk-screening death in a world where things don't turn out as they might or ought—planes crash, "129 Die in Jet!" from the *New York Mirror*, 1962. Your uncle's in the quicksand. Your mother's house burns to the ground. Your sister dies in her arms. You dig your own _____ and then you jump in. Someone else can fill in the _____. Eliot wrote about Poe: He had "an irresponsibility towards the meaning of words." But "when you do something exactly wrong," replies Andy on Poe's behalf, "you always turn up something." Were you talking, Andy, about your work, or some moral code from a long-forgotten world? I guess what I'm really trying to say is this: I was so imprecise, I had to say everything twice, and the world was, too. It was wonderful. The second time, everything was always new. Speaking was a revelation. Everything was a revelation. At home the elderly lost control of their bowels; at school I learned about the colon. At church people prayed for their own attention. Or intention, whatever that was. (I invent half of what I should have heard.) And I lived in that space, between knowing and unknowing, the body and the violence it does to what it tries to represent, the feeling that there's nothing, not even a word, you can ever possess. *Our bog is dood*, the children lisped. That's Stevie Smith; go read that, too. And my son whose tongue betrays him, whose ancestors were shoved into a _____ in Babi Yar, who speaks to me now of *worlds* and *woods* and *words*, like once I spoke of Suzanne at the shore; well, it's hard to know, it's hard to say the difference, isn't it?, it's hard to be precise. Why try? What can we ever possess? Words, after all, are like woods: they are places to hide, worlds to explore. It's hard to tell, perhaps, but I think of that when I read of Julia knowing her countryside, hiding, hemmed in on all sides by so many hatreds, hatreds so many, so sure, so precise they blur, blend, become something more, making, finally, together, no sense, which is to say, they become, in the end, history; I think of that when I think of Andy silk-screening death, of returning to Europe because Europe understood something America could not, about accidents and art and that *things fall apart* like that album cover by The Roots in 1999, a Black woman running, police in pursuit, the ghost of Yeats, the ghost of Achebe, the uncommon tongue, an image that needs to be repeated because it can't be understood, and can't be undone, because history is a gyre and *the gyre is wide as fuck.* That's what I thought when I scissored the two selections together.

On St. Leonard

The tribute concert to Leonard Cohen was led by a Canadian musician named (incredibly, to me) Li'l Andy, a 6-foot-4 country singer who told the *New York Times* weeks later this: "The reverence for Cohen has become a fully fledged civic mania." It has. It is. There are giant murals. Go and see for yourself. The *Times* piece is titled: "Is Leonard Cohen the New Secular Saint of Montreal?" The recording of Cohen reading came from the film *Ladies and Gentlemen, Mr. Leonard Cohen* (1965), which features the performance of "The only tourist in Havana turns his thoughts homeward." The poem begins: "Come, my brothers, / let us govern Canada. . . ." Let us. A parody of civic address by the poet, but not just that. "I was so I / And you were so you," late St. Leonard reminds us. But maybe now that's through. And we can give us a try. Let us. Let's. Let's go. Cohen's pop poems hold up. They did that night. People laughed. And cried.

On getting out of your head by looking through a skull

The imagined conversation between Warhol and Duchamp draws on things both artists said. Just not to each other. But things they said in the 1960s. And, yes, a mirror was part of the early planning stages for Duchamp, but at some point the mirror was dropped. Light breaks in. The door, some say, is really your skull. "The holes in the door are like the holes in our skull. . . . Duchamp calls attention to our own physical construct, our own bodily frame, a frame we carry with us always. We cannot get outside ourselves." And yet, we do, don't we?—precisely by feeling those limits, the mortal engine of pop's forms. Jonathan Safran Foer agrees—has Oskar play Yorick's skull in the school play. Skull play. The quote above is from an architect in "Duchamp's Doors and Windows." Heady, how so many thinkers in so many disciplines find so much in Duchamp. "Dead Poets" is dedicated to Sam See and to poets and thinkers and all sorts of artists like him who've let me get outside my head and share burdens with others. I cite Caroline Levine's *Forms: Whole, Rhythm, Hierarchy, Network* (2015), but lots of ghosts of influence are here. Some with names. Many without.

On Virginia Woolf at the movies

Woolf's essay "The Cinema" was prompted, in part, by watching *The Cabinet of Dr. Caligari* (1920), the German film some artists thought had ruined cinema (turning it back to theatrical stagecraft); others disagreed. It was popular, that's for sure, selling out theaters in re-release through the 1920s as a kind of throwback treat (but not just that) when Woolf finally caught it. You just had to see it! Of course, some Americans talked boycott, embargo, felt threatened at first sight. But not all. Some were up for a fight. The filmmakers behind *Manhatta* we meet in Section Four planned "to do in a scenic with natural objects what in *The Cabinet of Dr. Caligari* was done with painted sets." This was a putdown, of course, a rivalry, tough talk. But then again, perhaps we should talk "seriously of mocker's seriousness," like Stephen and his library friends in *Ulysses*. Does *Manhatta* repeat and redeem *Caligari*? In a way I think they thought it did. Find on the surface of things—in natural objects, outside!—new depths that Robert Wiene must rely on *painted sets* to convey. Isn't that what these Americans wanted? Anyway, if we get this rivalry, then Woolf's essay is funny (sort of) because she's distracted by something wrong (or right?) on the surface of the screen as she watches *Caligari*. "The blob on the screen," some critics have called it; a distortion; a momentary accident; and this is pop, a ghost in the machine, surface stuff. "Blob," like *Bob Loblaw*, is a kind of pop word, isn't it? (That's the name of the law[yer] in the TV show *Arrested Development*, you'll remember.) We like when things swerve. Woolf does. But not when they get arrested, stuck. We want them to develop, grow, change. Curve. That's how a new light shines through. Through the nonsense. In the nonsense. (Late St. Leonard: "Stop at the surface / The surface is fine.") Here's Woolf looking at an accidental doodle, a graphic mistake, a kind of error from Andy-world; whatever it is, it's a putdown of *Caligari*, but also a dream of a different cinema, a different screen ("It swelled to an immense size, quivered, bulged"). Film is plotting against our need for plots, or at least Woolf hopes. So are the throwback films she watches along with *Caligari*. In the States, more at peace with the German film, the little cinema movement in the mid-1920s toured American avant-garde films (*Manhatta*, for example) with *Caligari* during its re-release. Thrown into this mix was film history. This, actually, was when film history started in the US. We have an art. Right here. Look. Pop. (*Caligari* made the artists look.) Made them remember early Chaplin and early cinema. A kick in the pants! The Tramp! Take the machine into your hands! Amateurs, revolt! Everything becomes new again in light of the usual fare. The past always becomes new. Always. Always. You just have to wait for it. Scorsese would have felt right at home. Hugo, too.

On selfies as folk art

2013 became "the year of the selfie," according to some reports, but Philip Larkin's own photography, some two hundred images, emerged in 2015 with *The Importance of Elsewhere.* Maybe the importance is elsewhere, maybe we're moving away from selfies, maybe Larkin's work was a strategic counterpoint to Kim Kardashian's book of selfies, *Selfish* (2015)? Maybe. Actually, no. There are lots of photos of Philip there (in one he holds a wicker bunny). Funny, the photos gave a wider, gentler view of Larkin, like a Duane Michals portrait might do. "Kinder, softer, more receptive and intimate." Not exactly Larkin modifiers but photography can do that, too. Maybe a redemption not of the self but of the selfie is underway (one prays). Do these forms of self-portraiture seem less selfish? Maybe. Recently, I was stunned at an Inge Morath show; the photojournalist's touring exhibit gets bookended by two self-portraits that startle much like Freund's. Here is poise. The Morath exhibit ends as it begins but with a difference. It's hard to explain. I'll try. (But you'll have to go and see for yourself.) The original selfie she took as a young woman returns at the end of the show. They found it in her camera at her death. Her last photo. But the image is now changed, changed utterly. It's not the same. And yet, it is. She's done something to it. (You must see to believe.) It makes you think of how we revise, how we wait, a life, even, practice our art, stage, and stage again. Yes, it gets a bad rap, all of it. Selfies are energy and immediacy and instantly available and therefore true, say the critics, and sure that's true, but they've taught us, maybe, how to take our time, how to choose, and maybe stitch together parts, too, like Andy with his wounded parts, poor Frankenstein; how to choose the light, now this, now that, like a folk artist, like you're making a tapestry, even, fit for a queen, like Erin M. Riley, an artist who makes tapestries of selfies, selfie tapestries (you must look her up, too), weaving car crashes, and junk, and pop stuff, too—and these are all tapestries is the point, and maybe the only point of all of this, like a poet weaving reflections from the colors of the streets, like folk art, like Julia's art, making ourselves into something new, knitting together me and you, me and you; maybe that's what we want, maybe that's all that we want from pop, is to look down at the worsted flowers, like William Carlos Williams looking down at the worsted flowers, the worsted flowers beneath our feet, and see in the carpet shadows fluttering, see in the carpet a shadow of something, see in something somewhere something (of ourselves, a shadow of ourselves), and say we are the nightingales, and look up and say we are the nightingales, we are the nightingales, are we the nightingales, do you think?

Acknowledgments

Thanks to the *Los Angeles Review of Books* for permission to reprint these pieces that first appeared there in slightly different form:

"Wait for It: On Michael Robbins and Refrains" (November 16, 2017)
"After Winter: Leonard Cohen, Rostam, Noname" (April 23, 2018)
"Warhol's Mother's Pantry: Or, Pop in the Age of *Bird Box*" (February 26, 2019)

The two longer film essays at the end of the book also previously appeared but in very different form. Thanks to those presses for permission to reuse and repurpose this material:

"Early Cinema and the Post-9/11 City: *Hugo* and *Extremely Loud & Incredibly Close*," *The City Since 9/11: Literature, Film, Television*, ed. Keith Wilhite (Madison: Fairleigh Dickinson University Press, 2016): 245–260.

"'An Art That Won't Behave': Film and the *Seven Arts*, 1907–1921," *American Literature 84.1* (2012): 89–117. All rights reserved.

The Larkin section upcycles some material from "What to Do About the Teenage Philip Larkin?" in *Measure: A Review of Formal Poetry* 10.1 (Fall 2015): 52–67. A dance remix version appears in these pages.

The epigraph comes from brian g. gilmore's "portrait of black woman, exit 64, toledo, w/beautiful afro" in *come see about me, marvin*, published by Wayne State University Press (2019). Thanks to the poet for permission to use these lines.

Thanks to the team at The Ohio State University Press and Mad Creek Books. Thanks for selecting this work and seeing it through. Thank you for the Gournay Prize, and for encouraging writers to see what writing can do.

Support for this work came from the National Endowment for the Humanities, SUNY Plattsburgh, and UCLA.

I wrote a soundtrack for this book before I wrote the book itself. We recorded it in the old Pencil Factory in Greenpoint, Brooklyn (where the first colored pencils were made—equipment for doodlers: for Andy and Julia). ~~*WARHOLA*~~ by Famous Letter Writer. Go check it out. It's a record about pop. And memory. And the things that get erased. We learn to sing by singing along—with others. Through others. (Thanks to everyone who worked on those songs.)

And that leaves you: yeah, you. The reason I do what I do. This is for you. You know who you are (because you are I am).

21ST CENTURY ESSAYS

David Lazar and Patrick Madden, Series Editors

This series from Mad Creek Books is a vehicle to discover, publish, and promote some of the most daring, ingenious, and artistic nonfiction. This is the first and only major series that announces its focus on the essay—a genre whose plasticity, timelessness, popularity, and centrality to nonfiction writing make it especially important in the field of nonfiction literature. In addition to publishing the most interesting and innovative books of essays by American writers, the series publishes extraordinary international essayists and reprint works by neglected or forgotten essayists, voices that deserve to be heard, revived, and reprised. The series is a major addition to the possibilities of contemporary literary nonfiction, focusing on that central, frequently chimerical, and invariably supple form: The Essay.

*Warhol's Mother's Pantry: Art, America, and the Mom in Pop**
M. I. Devine

Don't Look Now: Things We Wish We Hadn't Seen
Edited by Kristen Iversen and David Lazar

How to Make a Slave and Other Essays
Jerald Walker

Just an Ordinary Woman Breathing
Julie Marie Wade

My Private Lennon: Explorations from a Fan Who Never Screamed
Sibbie O'Sullivan

*On Our Way Home from the Revolution: Reflections on Ukraine**
Sonya Bilocerkowycz

Echo's Fugue
Desirae Matherly

This One Will Hurt You
Paul Crenshaw

The Trouble with Men: Reflections on Sex, Love, Marriage, Porn, and Power
David Shields

*Fear Icons: Essays**
Kisha Lewellyn Schlegel

*Annual Gournay Prize Winner

Sustainability: A Love Story
Nicole Walker

Hummingbirds Between the Pages
Chris Arthur

Love's Long Line
Sophfronia Scott

The Real Life of the Parthenon
Patricia Vigderman

You, Me, and the Violence
Catherine Taylor

Curiouser and Curiouser: Essays
Nicholas Delbanco

Don't Come Back
Lina María Ferreira Cabeza-Vanegas

A Mother's Tale
Phillip Lopate